JAMESTOWN PUBLISHERS

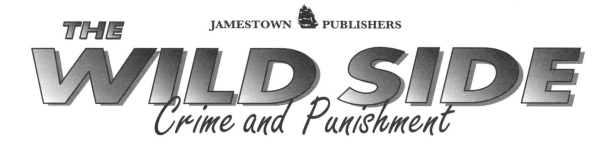

THE WILD SIDE
Crime and Punishment

JAMESTOWN 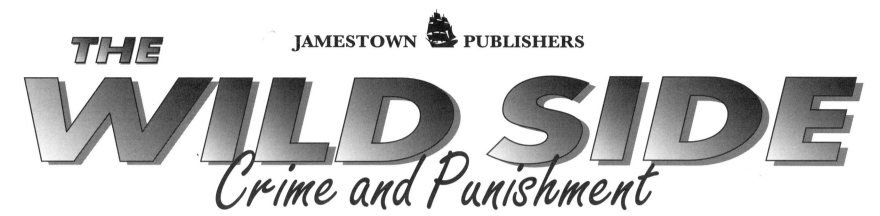 PUBLISHERS

THE WILD SIDE

Crime and Punishment

Henry Billings & Melissa Billings

JAMESTOWN  PUBLISHERS

a division of NTC/CONTEMPORARY PUBLISHING GROUP

Lincolnwood, Illinois USA

Photo Credits
Bettmann Archives: 16, 28, 34, 54
Tribune File Photos: 2, 4, 10, 22, 42, 48, 60, 66, 74, 80, 86, 92, 98

ISBN: 0-89061-799-6

Published by Jamestown Publishers,
a division of NTC/Contemporary Publishing Group, Inc.,
4255 West Touhy Avenue,
Lincolnwood (Chicago), Illinois 60646-1975 U.S.A.

90 DBH 987654

Executive Editor
Marilyn Cunningham

Editorial
Bob Green
Patricia Opaskar
Mary Ann Trost

Design and Production Manager
Norma Underwood

Cover Design
Michael Kelly

Production Artist
Thomas D. Scharf

Electronic Composition
Victoria A. Randall

Cover Illustration
Tim Jessell

Contents

GROUP THREE

To the Teacher

INTRODUCTION

We hear about crimes on the news every day. We seem to be hungry for all the details, we formulate our own opinions on the guilt or innocence of the accused, and often we vehemently agree or disagree with the sentence that is given to offenders. Although we deplore crime, we are also intrigued by it. In *Crime and Punishment*, students will take a close look at some of the most controversial and memorable crimes and criminals of the past two centuries. In some stories, students will have an opportunity to see the early, private lives that led to the public lives of crime. In others, they will read about the personalities and planning behind the crime. Still other stories raise questions that may never be answered fully. These high-interest stories capitalize on students' natural fascination with crime and punishment.

Crime and Punishment provides subject matter for thoughtful interpretation and discussion while challenging your students in four critical reading categories: main idea, important details, inferences, and vocabulary in context. *Crime and Punishment* can also help your students to improve their reading rates. Timed reading of the selections is optional, but many teachers find this an effective motivating device.

Crime and Punishment consists of fifteen units divided into three groups of five units each. All the stories in a group are on the same reading level. Group One is at the fourth-grade reading level, Group Two at the fifth, and Group Three at the sixth, as assessed by the Fry Formula for Estimating Readability.

HOW TO USE THIS BOOK

Introducing the Book. This text, when used creatively, can be an effective tool for teaching certain critical reading skills. We suggest that you begin by introducing the students to the contents and format of the book. Discuss the title. Encourage the students to think of some famous crimes they have heard of or read about. Have the crimes been solved to everyone's satisfaction, or do some people still have questions about them? Ask your students to recall crimes that have become topics of conversation across the country and around the world. Read through the table of contents as a class to gain an overview of the topics that will be covered.

The Sample Unit. Turn to the Sample Unit on pages 1–7. After you have examined these pages yourself, work through the Sample Unit with your students, so that they have a clear understanding of the purpose of the book and of how they are to use it.

The Sample Unit is set up exactly as the fifteen regular units are. The introductory page includes a photograph or illustration accompanied by a brief introduction to the story. The next page contains the story, which is followed by four types of comprehension exercises: Finding the Main Idea, Recalling Facts, Making Inferences, and Using Words Precisely.

Begin by having someone in the class read aloud the introduction. Then give the students a few moments to study the picture. Ask them to predict what the story will be about. Continue the discussion for a minute or so. Then have the students read the story. (You may wish to time the students' reading in order to help them increase their reading speed as well as their comprehension. Students can use the Words-per-Minute tables located on pages 110–112 to help them figure their reading speed.)

Next, work through the sample exercises as a class. At the beginning of each exercise are an explanation of the comprehension skill and directions for answering the questions. Make sure all the students understand how to complete the four different types of exercises and how to determine their scores. The correct answers and sample scores are printed in lighter type. Also, explanations of the correct answers are given for the sample Main Idea and Making Inferences exercises to help the students understand how to think through these question types.

As the students work through the Sample Unit, have them turn to the Words-per-Minute tables (if you have timed their reading) and the Reading Speed and Critical Reading Scores graphs on pages 113 and 114 at the appropriate points. Explain to the students the purpose of each feature and read the directions with them. Be sure they understand how to use the tables and graphs. You may need to help them find and mark their scores for the first several units.

Timing the Story. If you choose to time your students' reading, explain your reason for doing so: to help them track and increase their reading speed.

One way to time the reading is to have all the students in the class begin reading the story at the same time. After one minute has passed, write on the chalkboard the time that has elapsed. Update the time at ten-second intervals (1:00, 1:10, 1:20, etc.). Tell the students to copy down the last time shown on the chalkboard when they finish reading. They should then record this reading time in the space designated after the story.

Have the students use the Words-per-Minute tables to check their reading speed. They should then enter their reading speed on the appropriate Reading Speed graph on page 113. Graphing their reading times allows the students to keep track of increases in their reading speed.

Working Through Each Unit. When the students have carefully completed all parts of the Sample Unit, they should be ready to tackle the regular units. Begin each unit by having someone in the class read aloud the introduction to the story just as you did in the Sample Unit. Discuss the topic of the story and allow the students time to study the illustration.

Then have the students read the story. If you are timing the reading, have the students enter their reading time, find their reading speed, and record their speed on the Reading Speed graph after they have finished reading the story.

Next, direct the students to complete the four comprehension exercises without looking back at the story. When they have finished, go over the questions and answers with them. Have the students grade their own answers and make the necessary corrections. Then have them enter their Critical Reading Scores on the appropriate graph on page 114.

The Graphs. Students enjoy graphing their work. Graphs show, in a concrete and easily understandable way, how a student is progressing. Seeing a line of progressively rising scores gives students the incentive to continue striving for improvement.

Check the graphs regularly. This will allow you to establish a routine for reviewing each student's progress. Discuss with each student what the graphs show and what kind of progress you expect. Establish guidelines and warning signals so that students will know when to approach you for counseling and advice.

RELATED TEXTS

If you find that your students enjoy and benefit from the stories and skills exercises in *Crime and Punishment*, you may be interested in *Weird Science, Extreme Sports, Angry Animals, Bizarre Endings*, and *Total Panic*—five related Jamestown texts. All feature high-interest stories and work in four critical reading comprehension skills. As in *Crime and Punishment*, the units in those books are divided into three groups, at reading levels four, five, and six.

Sample Unit

Not long before his violent death, young William Bonney—also known as Billy the Kid—posed for this photo. According to legend, Billy killed at least one man for each of his twenty-one years. Sheriff Pat Garrett finally caught up to Billy at the home of a friend and killed him in a nighttime ambush.

THE LEGEND OF BILLY THE KID

Legend says that Billy the Kid killed one man for each of the twenty-one years of his life. That may or may not be true. Tales about this young outlaw are often overblown. It is hard to find the truth. Billy might have killed "only" nineteen or as many as twenty-seven men before he was gunned down in 1881. The exact number is not important. What is important is the way Billy stands out in history. Hundreds of books have been written about him. Most picture him as a romantic symbol of the Old West. But in fact, he was a heartless killer.

Billy the Kid was born William Bonney. He began his life of crime early. There was no school in his hometown of Silver City, New Mexico, so little Billy spent his time playing in the streets. He learned to gamble and to steal. He learned to fight with his fists. And he learned to use a gun.

The first man he killed was Frank Cahill. Apparently, Cahill called Billy a name. He was half joking. But Billy didn't think it was very funny. He hit Cahill. Then Cahill, a grown man, knocked fourteen-year-old Billy to the ground. That was a mistake. Flushed with anger, Billy drew his gun and shot Cahill.

Billy was put in jail, but he escaped a few nights later. He became a drifter. From time to time, he worked as a cowboy. He also made money playing cards. One night Billy accused a fellow gambler of cheating. The man just laughed at Billy, calling him a "billy goat." A moment later, the man was lying dead on the floor with a bullet hole between his eyes.

Billy's real killing spree began in 1878. He was nineteen years old. By then, he had hooked up with a man named John Tunstall. Tunstall, it was later said, was the Kid's one true friend. In fact, Billy called Tunstall "the only man that ever treated me [fairly]." Unfortunately, Tunstall had many enemies. One day a group of twenty-five men hunted him down. They shot him in cold blood. Billy witnessed the killing but was too far away to stop it. According to legend, Billy swore an oath at Tunstall's grave. "I'll get every [man] who helped kill John if it's the last thing I do."

Billy the Kid kept his word. He tracked down and shot every person who had played a part in Tunstall's death. One of these men was Sheriff William Brady. When Billy shot Brady, he gave himself a death sentence. He had killed a lawman. Now other lawmen came after him. They vowed to settle the score. Sheriff Pat Garrett tracked Billy for two years. In 1881 Garrett trapped him. Billy was arrested and brought to trial. He was found guilty of killing Brady. Judge Warren Bristol ordered Billy to be hanged until "you are dead, dead, dead."

But again Billy the Kid escaped. Fifteen days before he was supposed to be hanged, Billy somehow got his hands on a gun. He shot his guards. Then he took off into the New Mexico wilderness.

Sheriff Garrett formed a posse. He went after Billy again. For three months, he stalked him. At last, Garrett got a tip. He heard that Billy was staying at the Maxwell ranch near the town of Fort Sumner. Just past midnight on July 14, 1881, Garrett slipped into Maxwell's bedroom off the front porch. Billy, hearing noises, walked down the porch. He peeked into Maxwell's dark room.

"Who's that?" the Kid called out.

Garrett answered with two shots. The first bullet struck Billy just above the heart. The Kid died on the spot. Sheriff Garrett rushed out of the room, shouting, "I killed the Kid! I killed the Kid!"

If you have been timed while reading this selection, enter your reading time here. Then turn to the Words-per-Minute table on page 110 and look up your reading speed (words per minute). When you are working through the regular units, you will then enter your reading speed on the graph on page 113.

READING TIME: Sample Unit
_____ : _____
Minutes   *Seconds*

This photograph is thought to be that of William Bonney near the age of 18. If that claim is true, this would be only the second known image of Billy the Kid.

How Well Did You Read?

- *The four types of exercises that follow appear in each unit of this book. The directions for each type of exercise tell you how to mark your answers. In this Sample Unit, the answers are marked for you. Also, for the Finding the Main Idea and Making Inferences exercises, explanations of the answers are given to help you understand how to think through these question types. Read through these exercises carefully.*

- *When you have finished all four exercises in a unit, use the answer key that starts on page 105 to check your work. For each right answer, put a check mark (✓) on the line beside the box. For each wrong answer, write the correct answer on the line.*

- *Find your scores by following the directions after each exercise. In this unit, sample scores are entered as examples.*

A   FINDING THE MAIN IDEA

A good main idea statement answers two questions: it tells *who* or *what* is the subject of the story, and it answers the understood question *does what?* or *is what?* Look at the three statements below. One expresses the main idea of the story you just read. Another statement is *too broad*; it is vague and doesn't tell much about the topic of the story. The third statement is *too narrow*; it tells about only one part of the story.

Match the statements with the three answer choices below by writing the letter of each answer in the box in front of the statement it goes with.

M—Main Idea   B—Too Broad   N—Too Narrow

✓   N   1. When Billy killed Sheriff Brady, he attracted the attention of lawmen throughout the West. [This statement is true, but it is *too narrow*. It gives only one piece, or detail, from the story.]

✓   B   2. Gunfighters have become symbols of the Old West in the American mind. [This statement is *too broad*. The story is about a particular gunfighter, Billy the Kid.]

✓   M   3. Billy the Kid was responsible for many robberies and killings until the law finally caught up with him. [This is the *main idea*. It tells whom the story is about—Billy the Kid. It also tells you what he did.]

15   Score 15 points for a correct *M* answer.
10   Score 5 points for each correct *B* or *N* answer.

25   TOTAL SCORE: Finding the Main Idea

B RECALLING FACTS

How well do you remember the facts in the story you just read? Put an *x* in the box in front of the correct answer to each of the multiple-choice questions below.

1. One thing that Billy did NOT do as a boy was
   - ☐ a. learn how to use a gun.
   - ☐ b. learn how to gamble.
   - ✓ ☒ c. go to school.

2. According to legend, the first man Billy killed
   - ✓ ☒ a. had insulted Billy and knocked him down.
   - ☐ b. owed Billy money and wouldn't repay it.
   - ☐ c. drew his gun on Billy first.

3. It is said that the only true friend that Billy ever had was
   - ☐ a. William Brady.
   - ☐ b. Pat Garrett.
   - ✓ ☒ c. John Tunstall.

4. When Billy was found guilty of killing the sheriff, he was sentenced to be
   - ☐ a. shot by a firing squad.
   - ✓ ☒ b. hanged.
   - ☐ c. kept in prison for the rest of his life.

5. Billy was finally gunned down
   - ✓ ☒ a. at the Maxwell ranch near Fort Sumner.
   - ☐ b. in his hometown, Silver City.
   - ☐ c. as he escaped from prison.

Score 5 points for each correct answer.

__25__ TOTAL SCORE: Recalling Facts

C MAKING INFERENCES

When you use information from the text and your own experience to draw a conclusion that is not directly stated in the text, you are making an *inference*.

Below are five statements that may or may *not* be inferences based on the facts of the story. Write the letter *C* in the box in front of each statement that is a correct inference. Write the letter *F* in front of each faulty inference.

C—Correct Inference   F—Faulty Inference

1. ✓ 〔F〕 Most killers in the Old West were famous and popular. [This is a *faulty* inference. Just because one killer became famous does not mean that most did.]

2. ✓ 〔C〕 What Billy saw and learned on the streets of Silver City probably affected his actions as an adult. [This is a *correct* inference. You are told that Billy learned violent and illegal skills in the streets.]

3. ✓ 〔C〕 When Billy made up his mind to do something, he did it. [This is a *correct* inference. Billy kept his vow to kill those who had killed his friend.]

4. ✓ 〔C〕 Billy had a quick temper and often acted right away when he got angry. [This is a *correct* inference. The story states that Billy shot his victims just after they offended him.]

5. ✓ 〔F〕 When Sheriff Pat Garrett ran into problems, he usually gave up easily. [This is a *faulty* inference. Sheriff Garrett tracked Billy for years before finally catching up to him.]

Score 5 points for each correct *C* or *F* answer.

__25__ TOTAL SCORE: Making Inferences

D USING WORDS PRECISELY

Each numbered sentence below contains an underlined word or phrase from the story you have just read. Under the sentence are three definitions. One is a *synonym*, a word that means the same or almost the same thing as the underlined word: *big* and *large* are synonyms. One is an *antonym*, a word that has the opposite or nearly opposite meaning: *love* and *hate* are antonyms. One is an unrelated word; it has a completely *different* meaning than the underlined word. Match the definitions with the three answer choices by writing the letter that stands for each answer in the box in front of the definition it goes with.

S—Synonym   A—Antonym   D—Different

1. Tales about this young outlaw are often <u>overblown</u>.

   ✓ [A] a. understated
   ✓ [S] b. overdone
   ✓ [D] c. exciting

2. Most picture him as a <u>romantic</u> symbol of the Old West.

   ✓ [S] a. not based on fact
   ✓ [A] b. realistic
   ✓ [D] c. brave

3. He became a <u>drifter</u>.

   ✓ [A] a. person who likes to stay in one place
   ✓ [D] b. person who shoots well
   ✓ [S] c. person who travels aimlessly

4. For three months, he <u>stalked</u> Billy.

   ✓ [D] a. knew
   ✓ [A] b. avoided
   ✓ [S] c. followed

5. Billy <u>witnessed</u> the killing but was too far away to stop it.

   ✓ [S] a. saw
   ✓ [D] b. was sorry about
   ✓ [A] c. missed

15 Score 3 points for a correct *S* answer.
10 Score 1 point for each correct *A* or *D* answer.

25 TOTAL SCORE: Using Words Precisely

• *Enter the total score for each exercise in the spaces below. Then add the scores together to find your Critical Reading Score. Record your Critical Reading Score on the graph on page 114.*

_____	Finding the Main Idea
_____	Recalling Facts
_____	Making Inferences
_____	Using Words Precisely
_____	CRITICAL READING SCORE: Sample Unit

To the Student

Public Enemy Number One. The Ten Most Wanted list. Wanted: Dead or Alive. We hear these words, and chills run up our spines. Questions pop into our minds. What kind of crime was committed? Who did it? Where is the criminal now? When will he or she be caught? In *Crime and Punishment*, you will read about crimes and criminals that have been front-page news. Many of the people in these true stories simply fell into crime, while others planned their actions patiently and carefully. The criminals may shock you with their violence, their daring, their intelligence, their stupidity, or their dumb luck. The punishments they received may surprise or disgust you. But the stories will never bore you.

While you are enjoying these thought-provoking stories, you will be developing your reading skills. This book assumes that you already are a fairly good reader. *Crime and Punishment* is for students who want to read faster and to increase their understanding of what they read. If you complete all fifteen units—reading the stories and completing the exercises—you will surely increase your reading speed and improve your comprehension.

Group One

By 1933, Bonnie Parker and Clyde Barrow were already wanted by the law for many crimes. Yet they considered their deadly occupation the basis for horseplay. These fugitives on the run paused long enough to have a gang member photograph them playing with guns. Later, they abandoned the photos while escaping a raid.

BONNIE AND CLYDE

He was the "Texas Rattlesnake." She was "Suicide Sal." Together they drove through Texas, robbing and killing at every turn. They never got rich. In fact, they never managed to steal more than $1,500 at any one time. But they left a trail of blood across the land. It was this willingness to kill that made Bonnie and Clyde famous. From April 1932 until May 1934, they shot and killed a dozen people.

Bonnie Parker met Clyde Barrow in 1930. She was a nineteen-year-old waitress who was bored with life. She wanted excitement and danger. That was exactly what twenty-one-year-old Clyde seemed to offer. Clyde liked to gamble. He also liked to steal cars. When he needed money, he robbed stores or gas stations. Bonnie decided to hook up with him and have some "fun."

Unfortunately for Bonnie, Clyde wasn't a very good thief. At one break-in, he forgot to wear gloves. He left fingerprints all over the place. Soon after Bonnie met him, he was caught and sent to jail.

Bonnie could have walked away from Clyde right then. But she didn't.

She was in love with him. So she visited him in jail, slipping him a gun that she had taped to her leg. That night, Clyde busted out of jail. He was quickly recaptured, however, and sent to Eastman, one of the toughest prisons in the country. Clyde served two years there. When he got out, he was angry and bitter. He vowed never to spend another day in prison. "I'll die first," he declared.

Clyde meant what he said. With Bonnie at his side, he began robbing again. But now he was tougher. In fact, he was ruthless. He carried guns wherever he went. And he was ready to use them. On April 28, 1932, Clyde robbed a jewelry store in Hillsboro, Texas. He still wasn't a very smooth criminal, however, and during the robbery he panicked. He shot the sixty-five-year-old owner through the heart.

Now Clyde was a murderer as well as a thief. Still, Bonnie remained loyal to him. In fact, she became as cold and hard as he was. To her, killing became a kind of joke. She had Clyde take pictures of her holding a machine gun. In one photo, she pretended to

be robbing Clyde. In another, she and Clyde were both holding pistols and grinning wildly.

Like Clyde, Bonnie figured she would die young. She fully expected to be shot full of police bullets someday. That attitude earned her the nickname Suicide Sal. Bonnie actually wrote a poem by that title. The poem told the story of a woman who fell in love with a "professional killer." One part read:

I couldn't help loving him madly;
For him even now I would die.

Bonnie also wrote a poem called "The Story of Bonnie and Clyde." It included these lines:

They don't think they're too tough
   or desperate,
They know that the law always wins;
They've been shot at before,
But they do not ignore
That death is the wages of sin.

By the spring of 1933, Bonnie and Clyde had murdered seven people. They killed an old shopkeeper for $28. Clyde killed a sheriff and a deputy who spoke to him at a barn dance. Clyde shot one man on Christmas Day just so he could take a ride in the man's car.

That June, Bonnie and Clyde were traveling down a country road. Clyde was driving. He was usually an excellent driver. But on this day, he failed to see that a bridge was closed for repairs. He tried to stop at the last minute, but it was too late. The car flew over a steep bank, crashed, and exploded in a ball of fire. Clyde was thrown clear of the wreck. Bonnie, however, was trapped in the flames. By the time Clyde pulled her out, her whole body was badly burned.

Clyde took her to a nearby farmhouse. There a farmer's wife bandaged Bonnie as best she could. But Bonnie was in terrible pain. For a while, it looked as though she might die. Clyde nursed Bonnie all summer. He also continued to rob and kill. He rounded up some other thugs to help him. One was his brother, Buck.

That July, Buck was killed in a shoot-out with police. It happened at a park where the outlaws were camping. Clyde and Bonnie were there, too, but they managed to escape. Although Clyde was hit with four bullets, he did not fall. He helped Bonnie swim across a river. Then he stole a car and whisked her up into the hills.

Bonnie and Clyde spent the next few weeks in misery. Both of them needed medical attention. But they didn't dare go to a hospital. So, as Bonnie put it, "we lived in little ravines, secluded woods, down side roads for days that stretched into weeks. We were . . . so sick that time went by without our knowing it. We lost track of the days."

By September, Clyde was feeling better. He took Bonnie to visit her mother, Emma Parker. Mrs. Parker was horrified by her daughter's appearance. She said, "Bonnie was . . . unable to walk without help. She was miserably thin and much older. Her leg was drawn up under her. Her body was covered in scars."

Time was clearly running out for Bonnie and Clyde. Winter came. Still, the couple often had to sleep out in the open or in their unheated car. They moved from place to place, sticking to backwoods and small towns. By now, though, they weren't safe anywhere. A lawman named Frank Hamer was closing in on them.

In May of 1934, Hamer and his men set up an ambush near Gibland, Louisiana. On May 24, Bonnie and Clyde approached in a stolen car. Hamer's men shouted at them to halt. Said one officer, "We wished to give them a chance."

"But," added Hamer, "they both reached for their guns."

Before Bonnie or Clyde could get off a shot, officers blasted them with a total of 187 bullets.

Clyde slumped in his seat, dead. Bonnie, too, died instantly. The car crashed into a hillside. When Hamer and his men got to it, they found a machine gun lying in Bonnie's lap. Clyde's hand still rested on a sawed-off shotgun.

In the end, then, Bonnie Parker had been right. She had predicted this day would come. Her poem called "The Story of Bonnie and Clyde" concluded with these words:

> Some day they'll go down
>   together;
> And they'll bury them side by side;
>   To a few it'll be grief—
>   To the law a relief—
> But it's death for Bonnie and
>   Clyde.

If you have been timed while reading this selection, enter your reading time below. Then turn to the Words-per-Minute table on page 110 and look up your reading speed (words per minute). Enter your reading speed on the graph on page 113.

READING TIME: Unit 1	
_____ : _____	
Minutes	*Seconds*

How Well Did You Read?

- *Complete the four exercises that follow. The directions for each exercise will tell you how to mark your answers.*

- *When you have finished all four exercises, use the answer key on page 106 to check your work. For each right answer, put a check mark (✓) on the line beside the box. For each wrong answer, write the correct answer on the line.*

- *Follow the directions after each exercise to find your scores.*

A — FINDING THE MAIN IDEA

A good main idea statement answers two questions: it tells *who* or *what* is the subject of the story, and it answers the understood question *does what?* or *is what?* Look at the three statements below. One expresses the main idea of the story you just read. Another statement is *too broad*; it is vague and doesn't tell much about the topic of the story. The third statement is *too narrow*; it tells about only one part of the story.

Match the statements with the three answer choices below by writing the letter of each answer in the box in front of the statement it goes with.

M—Main Idea   B—Too Broad   N—Too Narrow

____ ☐ 1. Bonnie Parker and Clyde Barrrow were two of the most famous criminals in the United States during the 1930s.

____ ☐ 2. The murderers Bonnie Parker and Clyde Barrow were killed in a shower of bullets during an ambush by lawmen led by agent Frank Hamer.

____ ☐ 3. Although they were poor thieves, Bonnie Parker and Clyde Barrow became famous for their murdering ways and their loyalty to each other.

____ Score 15 points for a correct *M* answer.
____ Score 5 points for each correct *B* or *N* answer.

____ TOTAL SCORE: Finding the Main Idea

B RECALLING FACTS

How well do you remember the facts in the story you just read? Put an *x* in the box in front of the correct answer to each of the multiple-choice questions below.

1. Bonnie Parker first met Clyde Barrow
   - ☐ a. when he was nineteen years old.
   - ☐ b. when she was nineteen years old.
   - ☐ c. in 1919.

2. Clyde committed his first murder
   - ☐ a. during a jewelry store robbery.
   - ☐ b. in the course of a car theft.
   - ☐ c. when he broke out of jail with the gun Bonnie had brought him.

3. Bonnie wrote about her life as a criminal in
   - ☐ a. an autobiography published after her death.
   - ☐ b. letters to the editors of newspapers.
   - ☐ c. poems about herself and Clyde.

4. Bonnie was seriously injured
   - ☐ a. in a shoot-out at her mother's home.
   - ☐ b. in a fire caused by a car accident.
   - ☐ c. when she was playing with guns.

5. Before lawmen opened fire on Bonnie and Clyde,
   - ☐ a. the lawmen had a long conversation with them in an effort to get them to surrender.
   - ☐ b. the outlaws tried to run down the officers.
   - ☐ c. the lawmen saw them reach for their guns.

Score 5 points for each correct answer.

_____ TOTAL SCORE: Recalling Facts

C MAKING INFERENCES

When you use information from the text and your own experience to draw a conclusion that is not directly stated in the text, you are making an *inference*.

Below are five statements that may or may *not* be inferences based on the facts of the story. Write the letter *C* in the box in front of each statement that is a correct inference. Write the letter *F* in front of each faulty inference.

C—Correct Inference   F—Faulty Inference

1. If Bonnie had known that Clyde would become a killer, she would never have fallen in love with him.

2. Clyde Barrow became a criminal to impress Bonnie Parker.

3. Bonnie wrote poetry because she figured her readers would become sympathetic and would forgive she and Clyde for the crimes they committed.

4. Bonnie put her own mother in danger by coming to visit her.

5. If Frank Hamer's men had been more patient, Bonnie and Clyde probably would have surrendered peacefully.

Score 5 points for each correct *C* or *F* answer.

_____ TOTAL SCORE: Making Inferences

USING WORDS PRECISELY

Each numbered sentence below contains an underlined word or phrase from the story you have just read. Following the sentence are three definitions. One is a *synonym* for the underlined word, one is an *antonym*, and one has a completely *different* meaning than the underlined word.

For each definition, write the letter that stands for the correct answer in the box.

S—Synonym   A—Antonym   D—Different

1. In fact, he was <u>ruthless</u>.
   ____ ☐ a. merciless
   ____ ☐ b. helpless
   ____ ☐ c. kind

2. They don't think they're too tough or <u>desperate</u>.
   ____ ☐ a. hopeful
   ____ ☐ b. frantic, reckless
   ____ ☐ c. considerate

3. Then he stole a car and <u>whisked</u> her up into the hills.
   ____ ☐ a. slowly carried
   ____ ☐ b. whistled
   ____ ☐ c. quickly moved

4. So, as Bonnie put it, "we lived in little ravines, <u>secluded</u> woods, down side roads for days that stretched into weeks."
   ____ ☐ a. obvious
   ____ ☐ b. hidden, private
   ____ ☐ c. shady

5. Her poem called "The Story of Bonnie and Clyde" <u>concluded</u> with these words: ". . . it's death for Bonnie and Clyde."
   ____ ☐ a. began
   ____ ☐ b. sang
   ____ ☐ c. ended

____ Score 3 points for a correct *S* answer.
____ Score 1 point for each correct *A* or *D* answer.

____ TOTAL SCORE: Using Words Precisely

• *Enter the total score for each exercise in the spaces below. Then add the scores together to find your Critical Reading Score. Record your Critical Reading Score on the graph on page 114.*

_____	Finding the Main Idea
_____	Recalling Facts
_____	Making Inferences
_____	Using Words Precisely
_____	CRITICAL READING SCORE: Unit 1

During Prohibition, bootleggers feared government agents Izzy Einstein and Moe Smith, the two stout gentlemen on either side of this illegal still. This newpaper photo shows Izzy and Moe after yet another victory in their remarkable careers as agents enforcing New York City liquor laws.

IZZY AND MOE: TWO HONEST MEN

They had funny names: Izzy and Moe. And these two guys really *were* funny! People around the country laughed when they read about Izzy and Moe's latest tricks. It seemed that each new stunt was funnier than the last one. But Izzy and Moe were not a circus act or a comedy team. They were cops.

In 1919 a new law was passed. The law made it illegal to manufacture, sell, or transport liquor. This law was canceled in 1933. But for fourteen years, people were not allowed to use liquor. That meant beer and wine were out. So were gin, whiskey, and all other drinks containing alcohol. This time period was called *Prohibition.* That's because people were prohibited from having alcohol.

Many people ignored the new law. They thought it was wrong. They said the government had no right to deny them a bottle of beer or a glass of wine. Some people smuggled liquor into the country. These people were called *bootleggers*. Other people made their own booze—liquor—at home. "Bathtub gin" became a favorite. And all over America, people slipped into illegal bars called *speakeasies*.

Customers had to "speak easy" so they would not attract the attention of the police.

The police, meanwhile, were trying to enforce the law. That's where Izzy and Moe came in. Izzy Einstein and Moe Smith were government agents. Their job was to find people serving or drinking liquor and to arrest them. To do this, Izzy and Moe dressed in disguises. Some of their costumes were quite outrageous. They used smiles and laughs in order to trap bar owners. They were friendly with everyone—until it was time to make an arrest!

One night Izzy and Moe dressed up as football players. They knocked on a speakeasy door in New York City. "We won the game!" they shouted. "Let us in. We want to celebrate with a pint [of beer]."

The bar owner laughed and let them in. He praised them for their victory. Then he got them each a beer. But his smile quickly faded when Izzy and Moe flashed their badges. The two agents arrested the man for serving them liquor.

Then there was the time Izzy and

Moe wore dresses. Pretending to be ladies who had just come from the theater, they entered a restaurant. The two "ladies" ordered a small meal. All the time, their eyes scanned the restaurant. Izzy and Moe were looking for signs that the owner was selling liquor. They found plenty of clues. The next day, police raided the place. They found more than $10,000 worth of smuggled liquor.

Once Izzy and Moe dressed up as car mechanics. They found two hundred cases of whiskey in a garage. One time they dressed as grave diggers and raided a bar near a graveyard. Once they put on long black coats and carried violin cases. Their target? A bar that served only musicians. At times they also posed as horse traders, farmers, and rabbis.

Izzy and Moe's fame spread rapidly. "Be careful," bar owners would warn each other. "Izzy and Moe are in the neighborhood." Most owners came to hate these two agents.

Once Izzy walked into a bar alone. He looked up and saw his own photograph hanging over the bar. The owner had put black cloth around it to show that he wished Izzy were dead. Izzy went ahead and ordered a drink. It must not have been a very good photo of him, because the bartender didn't recognize him. Still, the man wouldn't pour Izzy a drink.

"I don't know you," the bartender said. (In those days, bartenders often refused to serve people they didn't know. They were worried about being caught by agents like Izzy and Moe.)

"Sure you know me," Izzy said. "I'm Izzy Epstein, the famous agent."

"You don't even have the name right," the bartender said with a laugh. "That guy's name is Einstein."

Izzy insisted that the name was Epstein. At last, he offered to bet the bartender a drink about it. The bartender agreed. He poured out two drinks. To settle the bet, Izzy pulled out his badge. He arrested the bartender on the spot.

Izzy and Moe came to the end of the line in 1925. They were dismissed from their jobs. The reason isn't clear. At the time, their bosses said Izzy and Moe had become too famous. Too many people recognized them. That meant they were no longer as useful as they had once been.

That might not have been the real reason. Some other agents resented Izzy and Moe's success. Still other agents feared their honesty. After all, some agents were crooks. They were paid by bootleggers to look the other way. Perhaps these crooked agents thought Izzy and Moe would find out about their deals. These agents might have arranged to get Izzy and Moe fired.

In any case, Izzy and Moe had built up quite a record. In four years, they arrested more than four thousand people. They also destroyed more than five million bottles of liquor!

If you have been timed while reading this selection, enter your reading time below. Then turn to the Words-per-Minute table on page 110 and look up your reading speed (words per minute). Enter your reading speed on the graph on page 113.

READING TIME: Unit 2

_____ : _____
Minutes   Seconds

How Well Did You Read?

- *Complete the four exercises that follow. The directions for each exercise will tell you how to mark your answers.*

- *When you have finished all four exercises, use the answer key on page 106 to check your work. For each right answer, put a check mark (✓) on the line beside the box. For each wrong answer, write the correct answer on the line.*

- *Follow the directions after each exercise to find your scores.*

 FINDING THE MAIN IDEA

A good main idea statement answers two questions: it tells *who* or *what* is the subject of the story, and it answers the understood question *does what?* or *is what?* Look at the three statements below. One expresses the main idea of the story you just read. Another statement is *too broad*; it is vague and doesn't tell much about the topic of the story. The third statement is *too narrow*; it tells about only one part of the story.

Match the statements with the three answer choices below by writing the letter of each answer in the box in front of the statement it goes with.

M—Main Idea   B—Too Broad   N—Too Narrow

____ ☐ 1. Izzy Einstein and Moe Smith dressed as women, rabbis, and farmers to trick bar owners.

____ ☐ 2. During Prohibition, Izzy Einstein and Moe Smith became famous across the United States.

____ ☐ 3. During Prohibition, Izzy Einstein and Moe Smith were colorful and effective government agents.

____ Score 15 points for a correct *M* answer.
____ Score 5 points for each correct *B* or *N* answer.

____ TOTAL SCORE: Finding the Main Idea

B RECALLING FACTS

How well do you remember the facts in the story you just read? Put an *x* in the box in front of the correct answer to each of the multiple-choice questions below.

1. During Prohibition, people were not allowed to
   - ☐ a. vote against liquor.
   - ☐ b. go to circus acts.
   - ☐ c. make, sell, or transport liquor.

2. Bootleggers were people who
   - ☐ a. smuggled liquor into the country.
   - ☐ b. made their own booze at home.
   - ☐ c. were customers at speakeasies.

3. Izzy and Moe dressed up in disguises in order to
   - ☐ a. get a great deal of publicity.
   - ☐ b. win prizes at contests at the bars.
   - ☐ c. trick people at bars and speakeasies.

4. Izzy's picture was hanging in one bar because
   - ☐ a. he was so well liked by the bar owner.
   - ☐ b. the bar owner wished he were dead.
   - ☐ c. he was quite a handsome man.

5. When Izzy and Moe lost their jobs with the government, their bosses said the reason was that they were too
   - ☐ a. honest.
   - ☐ b. famous.
   - ☐ c. old.

Score 5 points for each correct answer.

____ TOTAL SCORE: Recalling Facts

C MAKING INFERENCES

When you use information from the text and your own experience to draw a conclusion that is not directly stated in the text, you are making an *inference*.

Below are five statements that may or may *not* be inferences based on the facts of the story. Write the letter *C* in the box in front of each statement that is a correct inference. Write the letter *F* in front of each faulty inference.

C—Correct Inference   F—Faulty Inference

1. In general, U.S. citizens finally decided that a law against using liquor had little or no benefit.

2. The liquor used in speakeasies was almost always of poor quality.

3. Most of the people who broke the liquor laws during Prohibition had long criminal records.

4. During Prohibition, people who wanted a drink did not have a hard time finding bars that would serve them.

5. If Izzy and Moe had stayed on the job, they might have been in danger from their fellow agents.

Score 5 points for each correct *C* or *F* answer.

____ TOTAL SCORE: Making Inferences

D USING WORDS PRECISELY

Each numbered sentence below contains an underlined word or phrase from the story you have just read. Following the sentence are three definitions. One is a *synonym* for the underlined word, one is an *antonym*, and one has a completely *different* meaning than the underlined word.

For each definition, write the letter that stands for the correct answer in the box.

S—Synonym   A—Antonym   D—Different

1. That's because people were <u>prohibited from</u> having alcohol.

____ ☐ a. encouraged in

____ ☐ b. prevented from

____ ☐ c. made ill by

2. The police, meanwhile, were trying to <u>enforce</u> the law.

____ ☐ a. demand obedience to

____ ☐ b. get rid of, ignore

____ ☐ c. think about

3. Some of their costumes were quite <u>outrageous</u>.

____ ☐ a. expensive

____ ☐ b. strange

____ ☐ c. boring, not easily noticed

4. All the time, their eyes <u>scanned</u> the restaurant.

____ ☐ a. shut out

____ ☐ b. blinked inside

____ ☐ c. checked over

5. They were <u>dismissed from</u> their jobs.

____ ☐ a. fired from

____ ☐ b. given ratings at

____ ☐ c. employed at

____ Score 3 points for a correct *S* answer.
____ Score 1 point for each correct *A* or *D* answer.

____ TOTAL SCORE: Using Words Precisely

• *Enter the total score for each exercise in the spaces below. Then add the scores together to find your Critical Reading Score. Record your Critical Reading Score on the graph on page 114.*

_____ Finding the Main Idea
_____ Recalling Facts
_____ Making Inferences
_____ Using Words Precisely

_____ CRITICAL READING SCORE: Unit 2

At first, no one believed that John Paul Getty III, grandson of the richest man in the world, had been kidnapped. Even the ransom note didn't convince relatives and police. After all, the young man had recently suggested to friends that a fake kidnapping would be a great source of funds for his high living. Then a grisly envelope arrived, and everything changed.

THE KIDNAPPING OF JOHN PAUL GETTY III

Italian police thought it was a hoax. They did not believe sixteen-year-old John Paul Getty III had been kidnapped. A ransom note had been sent to Getty's mother. But it did not convince them. The note read:

Dear Mother:
   I have fallen into the hands of kidnappers. Don't let me be killed! Make sure that the police do not interfere. You must absolutely not take this as a joke.

The note then demanded $17 million for the boy's safe return.

Police had reasons to be dubious. Getty's grandfather was the richest man in the world. Yet young Paul was always running out of money. Neither his father nor his grandfather would give him the cash he wanted. Paul himself had never earned any money on his own. He had dropped out of high school. He had no job. His idea of a tough day was going to a big party. Just before he disappeared, he joked about his lack of funds. He knew of a way to solve his money problems, he told friends with a laugh. All he had to do was stage his own "perfect kidnapping."

That explains why police were not too alarmed when he disappeared on July 10, 1973. They did investigate, of course. They looked around. They asked a few questions. But privately they thought the whole thing had been set up by Paul. They waited to see what Grandfather Getty would do. Would he come up with money to "save" his missing grandson?

Old Mr. Getty answered that question right away. "I'm against paying any money," he snapped. "It only encourages kidnappers." These words upset Gail Getty, mother of the missing boy. She believed her son was in real danger. "At first I thought it might be a stupid joke," she told one person. "But then I understood it was serious." With old Mr. Getty refusing to help, Gail feared her son might soon be killed. She announced that she would try to raise the ransom money herself.

But Gail did not have that kind of cash. She was divorced from John Paul Getty, Jr. So she couldn't get her hands on the Getty fortune. Meanwhile, her ex-husband agreed with his father. No money would be paid out.

The weeks dragged by. Then, in November, something happened that changed everything. An envelope was sent to an Italian newspaper. When employees opened it, they found a gruesome sight. The envelope contained a note, a lock of Paul's red hair, and a human ear.

"This is Paul's first ear," read the note. "If within ten days the family still believes that this is a joke mounted by him, then the other ear will arrive. In other words, he will arrive in little bits."

Medical experts checked out the ear. It *was* Paul's. The boy's father and grandfather were shocked. They now realized that the kidnapping was real. Fearing for Paul's life, they agreed to bargain with the kidnappers. They would not pay $17 million, they said. But they would hand over $2.8 million.

The kidnappers took that deal. They told the Getty family to put the money in three plastic bags. These bags were to be left along the side of a road in southern Italy. The Gettys did this. But first they had the police photograph each bill. That way the money could be traced. After the ransom money was delivered, the Gettys sat back to wait. They hoped and prayed that Paul would be returned to them.

On December 14, Gail Getty got a late-night phone call from the kidnappers. They had received the money, they said. They were about to release her son. Early the next morning, a truck driver named Antonio Tedesco saw a young man standing by the side of the road. It was raining hard. Yet the young man was not wearing a raincoat. He was standing in wet clothes, waving his arms wildly. Tedesco slowed down. He saw that the young man was crying. As Tedesco pulled to a stop, the youth staggered over to the truck.

"I am Paul Getty," he said.

And so, five months after being kidnapped, John Paul Getty III was free. It turned out that he had suffered greatly during his five months as a hostage. The kidnappers had kept him blindfolded most of the time. They had forced him to march from one mountain hideout to the next. These long treks had exhausted him. Cold, frightened, and poorly fed, he had grown very weak.

Worst of all had been the ear episode. The kidnappers had tried to knock him out before they cut off his ear. "They struck me on the head to make me unconscious," he said. "But I felt everything. It was terrible."

With Paul safe, the police turned their attention to catching the kidnappers. Undercover officers had seen men pick up the ransom money. So the police knew who the kidnappers were. In late January 1974, police made their move. They arrested all eight kidnappers. And so the kidnappers did not get to enjoy much of the Getty money. It had been the highest ransom ever paid out in Italy. But as these kidnappers discovered, they had to return the money *and* go to jail.

If you have been timed while reading this selection, enter your reading time below. Then turn to the Words-per-Minute table on page 110 and look up your reading speed (words per minute). Enter your reading speed on the graph on page 113.

READING TIME: Unit 3
_____ : _____
Minutes   *Seconds*

How Well Did You Read?

- *Complete the four exercises that follow. The directions for each exercise will tell you how to mark your answers.*

- *When you have finished all four exercises, use the answer key on page 106 to check your work. For each right answer, put a check mark (✓) on the line beside the box. For each wrong answer, write the correct answer on the line.*

- *Follow the directions after each exercise to find your scores.*

A FINDING THE MAIN IDEA

A good main idea statement answers two questions: it tells *who* or *what* is the subject of the story, and it answers the understood question *does what?* or *is what?* Look at the three statements below. One expresses the main idea of the story you just read. Another statement is *too broad*; it is vague and doesn't tell much about the topic of the story. The third statement is *too narrow*; it tells about only one part of the story.

Match the statements with the three answer choices below by writing the letter of each answer in the box in front of the statement it goes with.

M—Main Idea   B—Too Broad   N—Too Narrow

____ ☐ 1. When the grandson of the world's richest man was kidnapped, the result was pain for the young man but no gain for the kidnappers.

____ ☐ 2. Nobody believed that young John Paul Getty had been kidnapped until the kidnappers sent a newspaper an envelope holding his ear.

____ ☐ 3. As the experience of John Paul Getty III showed, members of rich families are always in danger of kidnapping.

____ Score 15 points for a correct *M* answer.
____ Score 5 points for each correct *B* or *N* answer.

____ TOTAL SCORE: Finding the Main Idea

B RECALLING FACTS

How well do you remember the facts in the story you just read? Put an *x* in the box in front of the correct answer to each of the multiple-choice questions below.

1. The kidnappers of John Paul Getty III
   - ☐ a. demanded a ransom of $17 million.
   - ☐ b. sent a ransom note to his grandfather.
   - ☐ c. threatened the Italian government.

2. Police doubted the kidnapping was real because
   - ☐ a. the ransom note looked like a fake.
   - ☐ b. young Getty had been sighted around town.
   - ☐ c. young Getty had joked about faking his own kidnapping.

3. At first, the only person who agreed to pay the ransom was
   - ☐ a. John Paul Getty, Sr.
   - ☐ b. John Paul Getty, Jr.
   - ☐ c. the mother of John Paul Getty III.

4. Later, Paul's family agreed to pay
   - ☐ a. less than $3 million in ransom.
   - ☐ b. what the kidnappers had asked at first.
   - ☐ c. anything the kidnappers wanted.

5. After the ransom was paid,
   - ☐ a. Paul escaped from his kidnappers.
   - ☐ b. the kidnappers freed Paul.
   - ☐ c. the police freed Paul from the kidnappers.

Score 5 points for each correct answer.

____ TOTAL SCORE: Recalling Facts

C MAKING INFERENCES

When you use information from the text and your own experience to draw a conclusion that is not directly stated in the text, you are making an *inference*.

Below are five statements that may or may *not* be inferences based on the facts of the story. Write the letter *C* in the box in front of each statement that is a correct inference. Write the letter *F* in front of each faulty inference.

C—Correct Inference   F—Faulty Inference

1. Even members of rich families do not get to spend money as they like.

2. Paul's jokes about staging his own kidnapping probably gave the idea to the kidnappers.

3. Kidnappers may settle for a smaller ransom than they first demand.

4. If Paul Getty had tried to escape, he could have gotten away from his kidnappers easily.

5. It was only through chance, not ability, that the police caught the kidnappers of Paul Getty.

Score 5 points for each correct *C* or *F* answer.

____ TOTAL SCORE: Making Inferences

D USING WORDS PRECISELY

Each numbered sentence below contains an underlined word or phrase from the story you have just read. Following the sentence are three definitions. One is a *synonym* for the underlined word, one is an *antonym*, and one has a completely *different* meaning than the underlined word.

For each definition, write the letter that stands for the correct answer in the box.

S—Synonym   A—Antonym   D—Different

1. Italian police thought it was a <u>hoax</u>.
   ____ ☐ a. lie
   ____ ☐ b. adventure
   ____ ☐ c. reality

2. Police had reasons to be <u>dubious</u>.
   ____ ☐ a. trusting
   ____ ☐ b. displeased
   ____ ☐ c. suspicious

3. All he had to do was <u>stage</u> his own "perfect kidnapping."
   ____ ☐ a. fake
   ____ ☐ b. observe
   ____ ☐ c. send

4. When employees opened it, they found a <u>gruesome</u> sight.
   ____ ☐ a. pretty
   ____ ☐ b. grisly
   ____ ☐ c. familiar

5. These long <u>treks</u> had exhausted him.
   ____ ☐ a. tales
   ____ ☐ b. waits
   ____ ☐ c. journeys

____ Score 3 points for a correct *S* answer.
____ Score 1 point for each correct *A* or *D* answer.

____ TOTAL SCORE: Using Words Precisely

• *Enter the total score for each exercise in the spaces below. Then add the scores together to find your Critical Reading Score. Record your Critical Reading Score on the graph on page 114.*

_____ Finding the Main Idea
_____ Recalling Facts
_____ Making Inferences
_____ Using Words Precisely

_____ CRITICAL READING SCORE: Unit 3

Brink's armored trucks such as this one, filled with cash on the way to vaults, have been the target of many robbers. But one gang didn't stop at just the money carried on a single truck. They went straight to Brink's headquarters.

THE BRINK'S ROBBERY: THE "PERFECT" CRIME

Joseph "Big Joe" McGinnis dreamed of committing the perfect crime. In 1948 he hooked up with Tony "Fats" Pino. Pino shared McGinnis's dream. Together, these two longtime criminals set to work. They spent two years planning a flawless robbery. Nothing would be left to chance. No evidence would be left behind. And, if all went well, they would both end up rich.

The two thieves picked a tough target to rob—the Brink's Company in Boston. Brink's is an armored car service. It sends steel-plated cars to pick up money from stores around town. The armored cars take the money to Brink's headquarters. There it is counted, sorted, and held until the stores need it again. In 1950, as much as $10 million a day flowed through the Brink's office.

McGinnis and Pino planned their robbery with great care. They picked nine other men to join them. These were not just any nine men. Each brought a special skill to the group. Some, for instance, were good drivers or sharp lookout men. Also, seven of the men had to be *the same size*.

McGinnis and Pino chose men who were about five feet nine inches tall and weighed between 170 and 180 pounds. These men would be the ones to enter the Brink's office and bring out the money. They would all dress alike. They would wear the same scary masks, rubber-soled shoes, gloves, coats, and caps. That would make it hard for the Brink's guards to identify them. (McGinnis would be one of the seven, but Pino was too heavy for the job. He agreed to stay with the getaway truck.)

Robbing the Brink's headquarters would not be easy. The place was full of steel vaults and armed guards. McGinnis and Pino knew this. So they took plenty of time. They studied the layout of the building. They found out when the guards were on duty and where they were stationed. They watched the money flow in and out of the office. They knew when the big money was there.

One of the toughest problems they faced was the locks. The gang had to pass through five locked doors to get from the street to the Brink's office. McGinnis and Pino came up with a

bold plan. Late one night, a few of the gang members slipped into the building. One of them, a professional locksmith, removed the lock on the first door. He took it away and quickly made a key for it. Then—that same night—he hurried back to the Brink's building. He got the lock back in place before anyone noticed it was missing.

The robbers returned on four other nights. Each time they repeated their actions. They made keys for the locks on the four other doors. Now they would be able to walk right into the Brink's office. There, they knew, they would find guards standing inside a wire cage. That was where all the money was.

Next, McGinnis and Pino made the gang practice the robbery. More than twenty times, the thieves slipped into the building. They used their keys to unlock door after door. Each time, they got right up to the innermost door. Then they turned and left.

At last, McGinnis and Pino decided they were ready for the real thing. On January 17, 1950, they gave the signal. That night, a little before 7 P.M., the men took their places. Seven of them put on masks and sneaked into the building. They opened the five locked doors. At 7:10, they opened the innermost door. They were in the Brink's office. There, as expected, they saw five guards. The guards were all inside the wire cage, counting money.

The thieves stuck their guns through the holes in the cage. "This is a stickup," one growled. "Open the gate and don't give us any trouble." Thomas Lloyd, the head guard, looked at the seven drawn guns. He knew it was hopeless to put up a fight. He instructed one of the other guards to go ahead and open the cage door.

Inside the cage, the thieves ordered the guards to lie facedown on the floor. They tied the guards' hands behind their backs. In addition, they tied their feet together and put tape across their mouths. Then the crooks grabbed the money. They took all they could carry. In total, they stole more than 1,200 pounds in coins, bills, and checks. By 7:27 P.M. they were out of the building. The robbery had gone perfectly. In cash alone, they had made off with exactly $1,218,211.29!

When news of the heist spread, people were stunned. They hadn't thought anyone would ever dare rob Brink's. But, clearly, someone had. The police had no clues about who had done it. They searched everywhere. They organized a huge manhunt, but they didn't even know whom they were looking for. All they knew for sure was that the seven robbers were "of medium weight and height."

Meanwhile, the Brink's robbers played it safe. They drove the loot to the home of Jazz Maffie in nearby Roxbury. Then each man went back home to his family. The next day they all went to their regular day jobs as if nothing had happened. The thieves stayed calm. They waited a month before splitting up the money. Each man got about $100,000.

For six years, the police tried to solve the crime. They failed. But during that time, trouble was brewing inside the gang. One of the robbers did not like the way the money had been divided. Specs O'Keefe began demanding a larger share of the loot. McGinnis and the others became worried. They feared O'Keefe might go to the police. So they hired a gunman named Trigger Burke to kill him. One day Burke opened fire as O'Keefe drove by in his car. Luckily for O'Keefe—and unluckily for the rest of the gang—Burke missed his target.

Furious about the attack, O'Keefe did turn to the police. He told them the whole story. The police quickly rounded up all the Brink's robbers. The eleven men were brought to trial in 1956. All of them, including Specs O'Keefe, were found guilty. Since O'Keefe had helped solve the crime, however, police allowed him to go free. The rest of the gang got long prison terms. In the end, then, the dream of Big Joe McGinnis and Fats Pino had turned into a nightmare.

If you have been timed while reading this selection, enter your reading time below. Then turn to the Words-per-Minute table on page 110 and look up your reading speed (words per minute). Enter your reading speed on the graph on page 113.

READING TIME: Unit 4
_____ : _____
Minutes   *Seconds*

How Well Did You Read?

- *Complete the four exercises that follow. The directions for each exercise will tell you how to mark your answers.*

- *When you have finished all four exercises, use the answer key on page 106 to check your work. For each right answer, put a check mark (✓) on the line beside the box. For each wrong answer, write the correct answer on the line.*

- *Follow the directions after each exercise to find your scores.*

A FINDING THE MAIN IDEA

A good main idea statement answers two questions: it tells *who* or *what* is the subject of the story, and it answers the understood question *does what?* or *is what?* Look at the three statements below. One expresses the main idea of the story you just read. Another statement is *too broad*; it is vague and doesn't tell much about the topic of the story. The third statement is *too narrow*; it tells about only one part of the story.

Match the statements with the three answer choices below by writing the letter of each answer in the box in front of the statement it goes with.

M—Main Idea   B—Too Broad   N—Too Narrow

____ ☐ 1. The Brink's robbery took a long time to plan.

____ ☐ 2. The Brink's robbery is famous because it took great planning and the robbers left no clues.

____ ☐ 3. To help with their robbery, McGinnis and Pino chose skilled men of average height and weight.

____ Score 15 points for a correct *M* answer.
____ Score 5 points for each correct *B* or *N* answer.

____ TOTAL SCORE: Finding the Main Idea

B RECALLING FACTS

How well do you remember the facts in the story you just read? Put an *x* in the box in front of the correct answer to each of the multiple-choice questions below.

1. The target of the robbery was the Brink's Company in
   ____ ☐ a. New York City.
   ____ ☐ b. Los Angeles.
   ____ ☐ c. Boston.

2. Every day in 1950, the Brink's office handled about
   ____ ☐ a. $1 million.
   ____ ☐ b. $10 million.
   ____ ☐ c. $100 million.

3. Pino did not enter the Brink's office because
   ____ ☐ a. he was too heavy.
   ____ ☐ b. he was too nervous.
   ____ ☐ c. he was too tall.

4. When the thieves opened the innermost door of the Brink's office, they found
   ____ ☐ a. an armored car.
   ____ ☐ b. police waiting for them.
   ____ ☐ c. guards counting the money.

5. Six years after the robbery, Specs O'Keefe wanted
   ____ ☐ a. a bigger share of the money.
   ____ ☐ b. to tell newspaper reporters about his role in the robbery.
   ____ ☐ c. to kill the rest of the robbers.

Score 5 points for each correct answer.

____ TOTAL SCORE: Recalling Facts

C MAKING INFERENCES

When you use information from the text and your own experience to draw a conclusion that is not directly stated in the text, you are making an *inference*.

Below are five statements that may or may *not* be inferences based on the facts of the story. Write the letter *C* in the box in front of each statement that is a correct inference. Write the letter *F* in front of each faulty inference.

C—Correct Inference   F—Faulty Inference

____ ☐ 1. Joe McGinnis and Tony Pino trusted and worked well with each other.

____ ☐ 2. It would be easier to rob a regular car than it would be to rob an armored truck.

____ ☐ 3. The men who took part in the Brink's robbery were impatient and unable to keep a secret.

____ ☐ 4. The guards who did not resist the robbers were cowards.

____ ☐ 5. The robbers could have gotten away with the money even without a getaway vehicle.

Score 5 points for each correct C or F answer.

____ TOTAL SCORE: Making Inferences

D   USING WORDS PRECISELY

Each numbered sentence below contains an underlined word or phrase from the story you have just read. Following the sentence are three definitions. One is a *synonym* for the underlined word, one is an *antonym*, and one has a completely *different* meaning than the underlined word.

For each definition, write the letter that stands for the correct answer in the box.

S—Synonym   A—Antonym   D—Different

1. Together, these two longtime <u>criminals</u> set to work.

____ ☐ a. people who obey the law

____ ☐ b. people who know a lot about crimes

____ ☐ c. people who break laws

2. They spent two years planning a <u>flawless</u> robbery.

____ ☐ a. perfect

____ ☐ b. full of errors

____ ☐ c. difficult

3. Nothing would be left to <u>chance</u>.

____ ☐ a. the last moment

____ ☐ b. luck

____ ☐ c. planning

4. One of them, a <u>professional</u> locksmith, removed the lock on the first door.

____ ☐ a. without skill or experience

____ ☐ b. expert

____ ☐ c. talkative

5. <u>Furious</u> about the attack, O'Keefe did turn to the police.

____ ☐ a. extremely angry

____ ☐ b. surprised

____ ☐ c. happy

____ Score 3 points for a correct *S* answer.

____ Score 1 point for each correct *A* or *D* answer.

____ TOTAL SCORE: Using Words Precisely

• *Enter the total score for each exercise in the spaces below. Then add the scores together to find your Critical Reading Score. Record your Critical Reading Score on the graph on page 114.*

_____ Finding the Main Idea
_____ Recalling Facts
_____ Making Inferences
_____ Using Words Precisely

_____ CRITICAL READING SCORE: Unit 4

Some countries in the world punish wrongdoers in ways that we in America would consider cruel and unusual. In Pakistan, for example, a person convicted of a crime can be beaten in public. Some nations, such as Singapore, subject even their visitors to these punishments, as American Michael Fay learned.

PUNISHMENT, SINGAPORE STYLE

If you're thinking of committing a crime in Singapore, think again. This Asian country has some of the strictest laws in the world. There are laws against chewing gum and laws against spitting. You can be arrested for picking flowers or feeding the birds. You can even be arrested for not flushing a public toilet! And it's not just the laws that are harsh. It's the punishments, too. Penalties range from big fines to death by hanging.

Michael Fay was still a student when he moved to Singapore in 1992. He thought it would be great fun to spend his last two years of high school there. His mother and stepfather already lived in Singapore. So Michael went to live with them. Before he left the United States, his father told him to watch out. He warned Michael about Singapore's tough laws. "You're not in the U.S.," George Fay told his son. "Just keep that in mind."

But Michael Fay didn't listen. In Singapore, he fell in with a tough crowd. He hung out with kids who thought it was funny to go out at night and throw eggs at cars. One day in the fall of 1993, Fay was called into the principal's office. There, police were waiting for him. They accused him of spray-painting cars. They also accused him of stealing street signs.

Fay was taken to the police station and held there for several days. During that time, he admitted he was guilty. Later, though, his story changed. He said he only confessed after being slapped and punched by police. He said that the police had not allowed him to get enough sleep. They had worn him down until he was ready to admit to anything. Only then, he said, did he "confess." In a letter to his mother, he wrote, "I couldn't last anymore. I said, 'I admit to it.' They [the police] became nice to me from that stage on."

Fay hoped that the judge would take it easy on him. After all, he was just eighteen years old. He had no criminal record. Maybe, he thought, officials would just make him pay a fine. Maybe they would kick him out of the country. Being deported was fine with Fay. Singapore wasn't fun anymore.

But judges don't take it easy on lawbreakers in Singapore. Michael Fay was fined $2,200. He was given four months in jail. In addition, the judge sentenced him to be caned. That meant a guard would hit Fay with a cane six times across his bare bottom. And the guard would not be some ninety-pound weakling. He would be a martial arts expert, trained to inflict deep pain on the human body.

Caning is a common sentence in Singapore. But it caused an uproar in the United States. Some people thought it sounded cruel. Some even called it "torture." The cane that would be used was four feet long and half an inch thick. One stroke could rip open a person's flesh. A former head of Singapore's prisons described caning in vivid terms. He said, "The [guard] uses the whole of his body weight and not just the strength of his arm. After three strokes, the buttocks will be covered with blood."

Often, prisoners pass out during a caning. So officials have a doctor on the scene. The doctor's job is to revive the prisoner. Then the caning continues. The pain has caused many people to go into shock. Some cannot sit down or lie on their back for months afterward. One man got twelve lashes. He later said, "The pain burns in your mind long after it is over." And the scars left by a caning last forever.

After the sentence was announced, Fay's family went to U.S. President Bill Clinton. They asked for his help. Clinton issued "a strong protest" against the caning. He called the punishment "extreme." Clinton said that Singapore did, of course, have a right to enforce its own laws. But in this case, it was too much. Clinton did not think the punishment fit the crime.

Some Americans, though, approved of the caning. They thought Fay deserved what he got. Some even wished U.S. laws were more like Singapore's. Caning, they said, might help solve the crime problem in the United States. Even people in Fay's hometown of Dayton, Ohio, supported the caning. *The Dayton Daily News* said its mail was running strongly against Michael Fay. In a

phone call to his father, Fay asked, "Won't anybody hear me? I don't want to be caned."

If Fay got little sympathy in the United States, he got even less in Singapore. The people there take pride in their laws. They see themselves as tough on crime, not "soft," like Americans. Still, Fay tried an appeal to Singapore's Supreme Court. He was quickly turned down. The only good news Fay got came from Singapore's President Ong Teng Cheong. As a goodwill gesture to President Clinton, Ong Teng Cheong cut Fay's sentence down from six lashes to four.

And so on May 5, 1994, the guards took Fay to be flogged. They stripped off his clothes. They tied his wrists and ankles together. Then they bent him over a wooden frame. A guard gave Fay four swift and brutal strokes.

The caning opened up a two-inch gash. But Michael Fay did not go into shock. In fact, the Singapore government claimed that when it was all over, Fay "shook the caner's hand

and smiled." An angry George Fay called that a lie. "Mike's in pain," he said. Then he added, "But he's dealing with it OK."

The uproar over the caning died as quickly as it arose. President Clinton called it "a mistake." But he didn't do anything more. Still, the Michael Fay case taught Americans an important lesson. It's best to obey the law abroad as well as at home!

If you have been timed while reading this selection, enter your reading time below. Then turn to the Words-per-Minute table on page 110 and look up your reading speed (words per minute). Enter your reading speed on the graph on page 113.

READING TIME: Unit 5

_____ : _____
Minutes   *Seconds*

How Well Did You Read?

- *Complete the four exercises that follow. The directions for each exercise will tell you how to mark your answers.*

- *When you have finished all four exercises, use the answer key on page 106 to check your work. For each right answer, put a check mark (✓) on the line beside the box. For each wrong answer, write the correct answer on the line.*

- *Follow the directions after each exercise to find your scores.*

A FINDING THE MAIN IDEA

A good main idea statement answers two questions: it tells *who* or *what* is the subject of the story, and it answers the understood question *does what?* or *is what?* Look at the three statements below. One expresses the main idea of the story you just read. Another statement is *too broad*; it is vague and doesn't tell much about the topic of the story. The third statement is *too narrow*; it tells about only one part of the story.

Match the statements with the three answer choices below by writing the letter of each answer in the box in front of the statement it goes with.

M—Main Idea   B—Too Broad   N—Too Narrow

____ ☐ 1. Every nation creates its own set of laws as well as punishments.

____ ☐ 2. Michael Fay's family asked the president of the United States to help their son.

____ ☐ 3. Found guilty of a crime in Singapore, American Michael Fay was sentenced to caning, a punishment common there.

____ Score 15 points for a correct *M* answer.
____ Score 5 points for each correct *B* or *N* answer.

____ TOTAL SCORE: Finding the Main Idea

B RECALLING FACTS

How well do you remember the facts in the story you just read? Put an *x* in the box in front of the correct answer to each of the multiple-choice questions below.

1. Michael Fay was accused of the crime of
   - ☐ a. stealing cars.
   - ☐ b. feeding the birds illegally.
   - ☐ c. spray-painting cars.

2. The judge in Singapore sentenced Michael to
   - ☐ a. a caning.
   - ☐ b. hard labor in chains.
   - ☐ c. many hours of public service.

3. President Clinton called the punishment
   - ☐ a. "illegal".
   - ☐ b. "extreme".
   - ☐ c. "expected".

4. Public opinion ran strongly against Michael Fay in his hometown of
   - ☐ a. Chicago, Illinois.
   - ☐ b. Washington, D.C.
   - ☐ c. Dayton, Ohio.

5. As punishment, Michael Fay finally received
   - ☐ a. a suspended sentence.
   - ☐ b. four strokes with a cane.
   - ☐ c. twelve strokes with a cane.

Score 5 points for each correct answer.

_____ TOTAL SCORE: Recalling Facts

C MAKING INFERENCES

When you use information from the text and your own experience to draw a conclusion that is not directly stated in the text, you are making an *inference*.

Below are five statements that may or may *not* be inferences based on the facts of the story. Write the letter *C* in the box in front of each statement that is a correct inference. Write the letter *F* in front of each faulty inference.

C—Correct Inference   F—Faulty Inference

1. A complete knowledge of U.S. laws is important for people who are traveling to other countries.

2. In the United States, judges are often easy on first-time offenders and young people.

3. Citizens of the United States always support their fellow citizens in any disagreement with another country.

4. The president always becomes personally involved in any U.S. citizen's problems in a foreign country.

5. Michael Fay was probably eager for the day when he could leave Singapore.

Score 5 points for each correct *C* or *F* answer.

_____ TOTAL SCORE: Making Inferences

D · USING WORDS PRECISELY

Each numbered sentence below contains an underlined word or phrase from the story you have just read. Following the sentence are three definitions. One is a *synonym* for the underlined word, one is an *antonym*, and one has a completely *different* meaning than the underlined word.

For each definition, write the letter that stands for the correct answer in the box.

S—Synonym   A—Antonym   D—Different

1. And it's not just the laws that are <u>harsh</u>. It's the punishments, too.

____ ☐ a. old-fashioned

____ ☐ b. cruel

____ ☐ c. kind

2. <u>Penalties</u> range from big fines to death by hanging.

____ ☐ a. rewards

____ ☐ b. laws

____ ☐ c. punishments

3. If Fay got little <u>sympathy</u> in the United States, he got even less in Singapore.

____ ☐ a. indifference

____ ☐ b. pity

____ ☐ c. instruction

4. Being <u>deported</u> was fine with Fay.

____ ☐ a. jailed

____ ☐ b. invited into the country

____ ☐ c. ordered to leave the country

5. A former head of Singapore's prisons described caning in <u>vivid</u> terms.

____ ☐ a. colorful

____ ☐ b. sorrowful

____ ☐ c. colorless and bland

____ Score 3 points for a correct *S* answer.
____ Score 1 point for each correct *A* or *D* answer.

____ TOTAL SCORE: Using Words Precisely

• *Enter the total score for each exercise in the spaces below. Then add the scores together to find your Critical Reading Score. Record your Critical Reading Score on the graph on page 114.*

_____	Finding the Main Idea
_____	Recalling Facts
_____	Making Inferences
_____	Using Words Precisely
_____	CRITICAL READING SCORE: Unit 5

Group Two.

THE REAL JESSE JAMES

Jesse James is often pictured as a kind of modern-day Robin Hood. People talk about how he stole from the rich and gave to the poor. There have been songs, books, and movies about his heroic nature. But the real Jesse James was no hero. He was nothing but a thief and a killer.

Jesse Woodson James was born near Kearny, Missouri, in 1847. At the age of fifteen, he went to war. He fought on the side of the South in the Civil War. He was not, however, a regular soldier. Jesse joined a gang of raiders led by the cruel William Quantrill. They attacked and burned the homes of people who sided with the North. When the Civil War ended in 1865, the raiders broke up. Jesse and his older brother, Frank, went back to their farms.

No one knows for sure why Jesse and Frank turned to a life of crime. But they did. Maybe, after the thrill of war, farming seemed pretty dull. Jesse himself later blamed Northerners. He claimed Northerners who had taken over local banks refused to give loans to Southern farmers like himself. "We were driven to it," Jesse said. But that was a weak excuse. Jesse James didn't care about the fate of Southern farmers. After all, most of the people whom he robbed and killed were Southerners. There is no evidence that he ever gave a dime of stolen money to the poor—or to anyone else.

Early in 1866, Jesse became a member of an outlaw gang. His brother Frank was in the gang. So were several other old Quantrill raiders. On February 13, 1866, the gang robbed its first bank. The outlaws rode into Liberty, Missouri, in the middle of the day. A few went into the bank. They threatened to blow the bank teller's head off unless he gave them all the money.

Meanwhile, the other gang members kept watch outside. After the robbery, the outlaws jumped on their horses and headed out of town. In the street, they passed a college student named George Wymore. He was on his way to class. Seeing the riders thundering down the street, Wymore ran for cover. One of the gang members shot him in the back. He died instantly. It was the first of many times an innocent person was gunned down by this gang. Jesse soon showed he was the most daring of the gang members and the most willing to kill. People began to think of him as the gang's leader.

After each bank robbery, Jesse and the rest of the gang went into hiding. They waited for the public outrage to die down. It was usually many months before they hit another bank. Sometimes they passed the time by ambushing stagecoaches and robbing the passengers. Then, in 1873, the James gang found a much richer target—trains. That year they planned their first train robbery. They picked the Rock Island Express in Adair, Iowa. Jesse and the other men stopped the train by taking away a piece of the track. When engineer John Rafferty saw

In this photograph of business associates, all the men appear to be upstanding citizens. However, your town's chamber of commerce would not appreciate their membership. This is the James gang, a group of notorious bandits and killers.

the broken track, he threw his engine into reverse. It was too late. The train crashed onto its side, killing Rafferty. James and his gang made off with about $2,000.

By 1874 Jesse James was world famous. He added to his fame with the boldest train robbery up to that time. It took place in the small town of Gad's Hill, Missouri. Not only did Jesse's gang steal all the train's money, but they robbed everyone on board as well. The outlaws loved every minute of it. One grabbed the hat off a passenger's head. Another laughingly told a minister on board to pray for them. Jesse even wrote his own news story about the crime. He left it with a passenger, saying, "Give that to the editor of the St. Louis *Dispatch*." Since he hadn't counted the money yet, Jesse left a blank space for the amount of money stolen.

Jesse planned each raid carefully. He and his men struck by surprise. Often they met little or no resistance. That was because these former Civil War raiders knew how to terrorize people. Still, that did not always work. Sometimes the townspeople fought back. One day the gang tried to rob a bank in Savannah, Missouri. Led by a local judge, the citizens drove them away before the outlaws got a nickel. The gang later robbed a bank in

Richmond, Missouri. The citizens there formed a posse to chase them. The posse caught three of the robbers and lynched them from a nearby tree.

In 1876 the gang was nearly destroyed when the members tried to rob a bank in Northfield, Minnesota. Again they ran into some tough townsfolk. The outlaws tried to scare people by firing shots in the air. They hoped to stir up enough panic so they could make a clean getaway. But the townspeople knew what the gunshots meant. The bank was being robbed! Several citizens sprang into action. They grabbed their guns and took off after the gang. Only Jesse and Frank managed to escape. All the rest of the gang members were captured or killed.

Shaken, Jesse and Frank went into hiding. For weeks they dared travel only at night. They slept in barns and stayed alive by eating raw vegetables from the fields. For three years they kept a low profile. They waited for a chance to resume their life of crime.

At last, in 1879, Jesse put together a new gang. The robbing and killing began all over again. By this time, many people had had enough of Jesse. The reward for his capture or death kept mounting. Lots of men wanted to collect the reward. Jesse knew he had to be extra careful now.

Every member of the gang felt the pressure. Lawmen might be lurking behind any tree. They might be waiting around any corner. One gang member, Ed Miller, asked Jesse to give up. Jesse responded by shooting him. As it turned out, Jesse killed the wrong man. It was gang member Bob Ford who turned against Jesse. Ford went to see the governor of Missouri. No one ever found out what the governor promised him, but it must have been good. On April 3, 1882, Ford went to see Jesse at his cabin near St. Joseph, Missouri. While Jesse's back was turned, Ford pulled out his gun. He shot Jesse James in the back of the head. Some people were saddened by Jesse's death. But others were pleased to see the end of America's most famous outlaw.

If you have been timed while reading this selection, enter your reading time below. Then turn to the Words-per-Minute table on page 111 and look up your reading speed (words per minute). Enter your reading speed on the graph on page 113.

READING TIME: Unit 6
_____ : _____
Minutes   *Seconds*

How Well Did You Read?

- *Complete the four exercises that follow. The directions for each exercise will tell you how to mark your answers.*

- *When you have finished all four exercises, use the answer key on page 107 to check your work. For each right answer, put a check mark (✓) on the line beside the box. For each wrong answer, write the correct answer on the line.*

- *Follow the directions after each exercise to find your scores.*

A   FINDING THE MAIN IDEA

A good main idea statement answers two questions: it tells *who* or *what* is the subject of the story, and it answers the understood question *does what?* or *is what?* Look at the three statements below. One expresses the main idea of the story you just read. Another statement is *too broad*; it is vague and doesn't tell much about the topic of the story. The third statement is *too narrow*; it tells about only one part of the story.

Match the statements with the three answer choices below by writing the letter of each answer in the box in front of the statement it goes with.

M—Main Idea   B—Too Broad   N—Too Narrow

_____ ☐   1. Jesse James was a clever but heartless killer who led gangs in bank and train robberies until he was killed by one of his own men for a reward.

_____ ☐   2. Jesse James, a famous outlaw, was one of the many lawless men who roamed the American West after the Civil War.

_____ ☐   3. After most of his gang was caught or killed following an 1876 bank robbery, Jesse James hid for three years before resuming his life of crime.

_____   Score 15 points for a correct *M* answer.
_____   Score 5 points for each correct *B* or *N* answer.

_____   TOTAL SCORE: Finding the Main Idea

B RECALLING FACTS

How well do you remember the facts in the story you just read? Put an *x* in the box in front of the correct answer to each of the multiple-choice questions below.

1. During the Civil War, Jesse James fought
   - ____ ☐ a. in the infantry of the Union army.
   - ____ ☐ b. in the Confederate cavalry, under Sherman.
   - ____ ☐ c. for the South, with Quantrill's raiders.

2. Jesse's gang began by robbing
   - ____ ☐ a. stagecoaches.
   - ____ ☐ b. trains.
   - ____ ☐ c. banks.

3. In the James gang's first train robbery, the engineer was killed
   - ____ ☐ a. in the train wreck that the gang caused.
   - ____ ☐ b. by gunfire when the gang attacked.
   - ____ ☐ c. when he refused to cooperate.

4. When the James gang left the Missouri area to rob a bank in Minnesota, the Minnesota townspeople
   - ____ ☐ a. caught or killed all but the James brothers.
   - ____ ☐ b. were too frightened to resist.
   - ____ ☐ c. were happy to have a famous outlaw visit.

5. Jesse died
   - ____ ☐ a. while running from a bungled bank job.
   - ____ ☐ b. while at home in Missouri.
   - ____ ☐ c. by hanging after a short trial.

Score 5 points for each correct answer.

____ TOTAL SCORE: Recalling Facts

C MAKING INFERENCES

When you use information from the text and your own experience to draw a conclusion that is not directly stated in the text, you are making an *inference*.

Below are five statements that may or may *not* be inferences based on the facts of the story. Write the letter *C* in the box in front of each statement that is a correct inference. Write the letter *F* in front of each faulty inference.

C—Correct Inference   F—Faulty Inference

- ____ ☐ 1. Many legends about so-called heroes of the American West have little connection with the facts.

- ____ ☐ 2. After the Civil War, most former Confederate soldiers turned to lives of crime.

- ____ ☐ 3. Jesse James and his gang enjoyed getting publicity for their crimes.

- ____ ☐ 4. In small towns of the late 1800s, citizens relied entirely on their police forces to maintain order.

- ____ ☐ 5. Some members of Jesse's second, or new, gang did not really respect or admire Jesse.

Score 5 points for each correct *C* or *F* answer.

____ TOTAL SCORE: Making Inferences

D USING WORDS PRECISELY

Each numbered sentence below contains an underlined word or phrase from the story you have just read. Following the sentence are three definitions. One is a *synonym* for the underlined word, one is an *antonym*, and one has a completely *different* meaning than the underlined word.

For each definition, write the letter that stands for the correct answer in the box.

S—Synonym   A—Antonym   D—Different

1. There have been songs, books, and movies about his <u>heroic</u> nature.

____ ☐ a. brave and noble

____ ☐ b. cowardly

____ ☐ c. stylish

2. For three years they <u>kept a low profile</u>.

____ ☐ a. showed off

____ ☐ b. behaved quietly so as to avoid notice

____ ☐ c. stayed on a diet

3. The reward for his capture or death kept <u>mounting</u>.

____ ☐ a. calling

____ ☐ b. falling

____ ☐ c. rising

4. He and his men struck by surprise. Often they met little or no <u>resistance</u>.

____ ☐ a. giving in

____ ☐ b. ability

____ ☐ c. opposition

5. They hoped to stir up enough <u>panic</u> so they could make a clean getaway.

____ ☐ a. interest

____ ☐ b. sudden, widespread terror

____ ☐ c. calmness

____ Score 3 points for a correct *S* answer.
____ Score 1 point for each correct *A* or *D* answer.

____ TOTAL SCORE: Using Words Precisely

• *Enter the total score for each exercise in the spaces below. Then add the scores together to find your Critical Reading Score. Record your Critical Reading Score on the graph on page 114.*

_____ Finding the Main Idea
_____ Recalling Facts
_____ Making Inferences
_____ Using Words Precisely

_____ CRITICAL READING SCORE: Unit 6

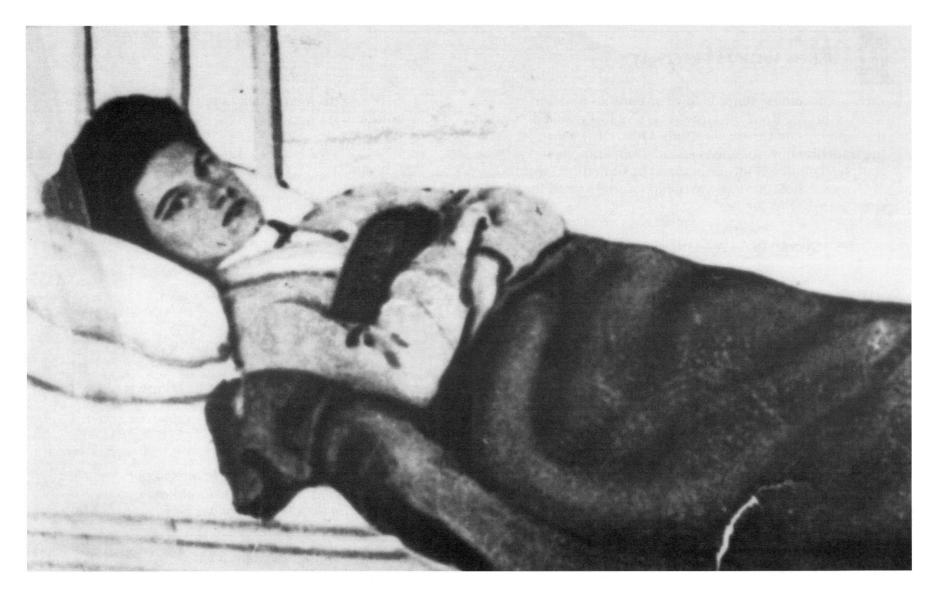

Confined in a hospital for testing, Mary Mallon glares defiantly at the photographer. This handsome, attractive woman never believed what the medical tests revealed—that she was the carrier of typhoid bacteria that killed many people who ate her cooking.

TYPHOID MARY

Mary Mallon didn't mean to kill people. For a long time, she didn't even realize she was doing it. All she knew was that wherever she went, people got sick. It was a pattern. She would be hired as a cook by a wealthy New York family. She would begin making meals. But within weeks, the family would come down with a horrible disease called *typhoid*.

The disease began with chills and a fever. Victims often felt sick to their stomach. They developed a headache and suffered from nosebleeds. Next, they broke out with a bright red rash. They began coughing. Sometimes the fever would break and they would recover. In other cases, their condition would worsen and they would die.

In the early 1900s few people understood how typhoid is spread. Some people thought it came from spoiled milk. Others thought it came from garbage fumes. Only a few scientists had figured out the truth: it is caused by germs that live inside the human body. These germs pass through the body when a person uses the toilet. Sometimes the germs get on a person's hands. If the person

touches food before washing up, the germs can be transferred to the food. Anyone who eats the food can then come down with the disease. In the early 1900s, about one out of every five people sick with typhoid died.

Mary Mallon had never had typhoid. She had always been healthy and strong. She had no reason to think she might be passing the disease on to anyone. And yet . . . no matter where she went, typhoid soon followed. Mary's reaction to this problem was simple. She ran away. Once she did stay and help nurse a family through the illness. But the rest of the time, she just packed her bags and moved on.

In 1906 Mary got a job as the cook for Charles Warren and his family. She had been with the Warrens just three weeks when one of the children got a fever. Mary knew what that meant. Typhoid had struck again. Quickly she collected her pay. Then she took off. But this time she was followed. A man named George Soper began investigating the Warren family's illness.

Soper was an expert on diseases. He knew how typhoid was spread. He figured that healthy people could carry typhoid germs around without knowing it. Perhaps, he thought, Mary Mallon was a carrier of these germs. He decided to track her down. He wanted to run tests to see if her body housed typhoid germs.

Soper found Mary in March of 1907. She was working as a cook for yet another New York family. As Soper had feared, a girl in the house was already dying of typhoid. Soper went to the house. Mary was in the kitchen. When Soper told her why he had come, she became furious. She picked up a huge carving fork and lunged at him. Soper managed to run away without being hurt.

Soon after that, Soper went to see where Mary lived. It was a dirty, smelly place. Standing in the filth, Soper understood how Mary could spread typhoid to so many people. She clearly had very poor health habits.

Soper sent Dr. Josephine Baker to talk to Mary. Baker worked for the city. It was her job to protect people from health hazards. But Baker had no luck, either. Mary simply did not believe what the doctor told her. It sounded crazy. After all, she was healthy. Surely she was not carrying typhoid around inside her body. Mary just wanted everyone to leave her alone. She wanted to go on earning a living as a cook. And as for washing her hands after using the toilet—well, that seemed like a waste of time and energy.

Baker and other city officials did not know what to do. At last they decided to lock Mary up. It was a desperate move. But no one could think of any other way to stop her from spreading typhoid. Baker and five police officers went to get her. When Mary saw them coming, she fled. After a two-hour search, she was found crouched in a neighbor's yard. When the police grabbed her, she began kicking and biting. It took all five officers to drag her into an ambulance. Said Dr. Baker, "I literally sat on her all the way to the hospital. It was like being in a cage with an angry lion."

Mary was kept at the hospital for months. As expected, tests showed that her body was full of typhoid germs. That fall, she was transferred to a hospital on a tiny island near the city. She was kept there for three years. She got a lawyer to help her fight for her freedom. She argued that it was illegal for the city to hold her prisoner. Mary was right, but no judge was willing to set her free. And so she remained locked up on North Brother Island.

In 1910 Mary finally agreed to do what the doctors wanted. If they let her go, she said, she would never work as a cook again. She also promised to check in with them every three months. Doctors agreed to the plan. They turned Mary loose. But as soon as she was back on the streets, she vanished. For five years, no city official could find her.

During that time, Mary floated from one restaurant job to the next. She cooked for hotels. She cooked in diners. She made up different names for herself. And she ran away whenever one of her customers got typhoid.

In 1915 Mary got a kitchen job at the Sloane Hospital for Women in New York City. Soon twenty-five people there came down with typhoid. One of the workers joked that the cook must be the infamous Typhoid Mary. Terrified of being caught again, Mary took off for New Jersey. But now police were on her trail. On May 27, 1915, she was arrested and returned to North Brother Island.

Mary Mallon had reached the end of the line. Health officials were not going to give her any more chances. They decided to keep her on that little island for the rest of her life. For twenty-two years, until her death at age seventy, that's where Mary stayed. In her later years, she was given her own cottage to live in. She could have visitors whenever she wanted. At mealtime, though, everyone knew what to do. They always left without eating a bite of Typhoid Mary's cooking.

If you have been timed while reading this selection, enter your reading time below. Then turn to the Words-per-Minute table on page 111 and look up your reading speed (words per minute). Enter your reading speed on the graph on page 113.

READING TIME: Unit 7

_____ : _____

Minutes   *Seconds*

How Well Did You Read?

- *Complete the four exercises that follow. The directions for each exercise will tell you how to mark your answers.*

- *When you have finished all four exercises, use the answer key on page 107 to check your work. For each right answer, put a check mark (✓) on the line beside the box. For each wrong answer, write the correct answer on the line.*

- *Follow the directions after each exercise to find your scores.*

A FINDING THE MAIN IDEA

A good main idea statement answers two questions: it tells *who* or *what* is the subject of the story, and it answers the understood question *does what?* or *is what?* Look at the three statements below. One expresses the main idea of the story you just read. Another statement is *too broad*; it is vague and doesn't tell much about the topic of the story. The third statement is *too narrow*; it tells about only one part of the story.

Match the statements with the three answer choices below by writing the letter of each answer in the box in front of the statement it goes with.

M—Main Idea   B—Too Broad   N—Too Narrow

_____ ☐ 1. George Soper was the first person to suspect that Mary Mallon might have caused the Warren family's illness.

_____ ☐ 2. Typhoid is a powerful disease that can cause grave illness and sometimes even death.

_____ ☐ 3. Mary Mallon carried deadly typhoid germs and infected many victims before she was arrested and put in a hospital.

_____ Score 15 points for a correct *M* answer.
_____ Score 5 points for each correct *B* or *N* answer.

_____ TOTAL SCORE: Finding the Main Idea

B RECALLING FACTS

How well do you remember the facts in the story you just read? Put an *x* in the box in front of the correct answer to each of the multiple-choice questions below.

1. Mary Mallon cooked for wealthy families in
   - ☐ a. New York.
   - ☐ b. Pennsylvania.
   - ☐ c. Florida.

2. Typhoid germs are carried around in
   - ☐ a. spoiled milk.
   - ☐ b. the human body.
   - ☐ c. garbage fumes.

3. Usually, when Mary's victims became ill, she
   - ☐ a. reported their illness to health officials.
   - ☐ b. nursed them back to health.
   - ☐ c. packed her bags and left.

4. It was hard for Mary to believe that she could spread typhoid because she
   - ☐ a. could not understand what typhoid was.
   - ☐ b. was very healthy herself.
   - ☐ c. did not even know that her victims were getting sick.

5. To get released, Mary agreed never to
   - ☐ a. work as a cook again.
   - ☐ b. make her home in New York.
   - ☐ c. leave the United States.

Score 5 points for each correct answer.

____ TOTAL SCORE: Recalling Facts

C MAKING INFERENCES

When you use information from the text and your own experience to draw a conclusion that is not directly stated in the text, you are making an *inference*.

Below are five statements that may or may *not* be inferences based on the facts of the story. Write the letter *C* in the box in front of each statement that is a correct inference. Write the letter *F* in front of each faulty inference.

C—Correct Inference   F—Faulty Inference

1. Mary Mallon was a gentle, honest person who would go to great lengths not to harm anyone.

2. In the early 1900s wealthy people often hired cooks to prepare their meals in their homes.

3. It is a good idea to make sure that all workers in restaurants wash their hands after they use the toilet.

4. As long as you feel healthy and strong, you can never be a carrier of typhoid germs.

5. Mary Mallon had extraordinary strength, especially when she was upset or angry.

Score 5 points for each correct *C* or *F* answer.

____ TOTAL SCORE: Making Inferences

D USING WORDS PRECISELY

Each numbered sentence below contains an underlined word or phrase from the story you have just read. Following the sentence are three definitions. One is a *synonym* for the underlined word, one is an *antonym*, and one has a completely *different* meaning than the underlined word.

For each definition, write the letter that stands for the correct answer in the box.

S—Synonym   A—Antonym   D—Different

1. Standing in the <u>filth</u>, Soper understood how Mary could spread typhoid to so many people.

____ ☐ a. dirt

____ ☐ b. purity

____ ☐ c. room

2. Sometimes the fever would break and they would <u>recover</u>.

____ ☐ a. become pale

____ ☐ b. get back to normal

____ ☐ c. worsen

3. All she knew was that wherever she went, people got sick. It was a <u>pattern</u>.

____ ☐ a. arrangement by chance

____ ☐ b. worry

____ ☐ c. set of repeating events or items

4. But as soon as she was back on the streets, she <u>vanished</u>.

____ ☐ a. understood

____ ☐ b. disappeared

____ ☐ c. reappeared

5. She picked up a huge carving fork and <u>lunged at</u> him.

____ ☐ a. backed away from

____ ☐ b. attacked

____ ☐ c. shouted at

____ Score 3 points for a correct *S* answer.

____ Score 1 point for each correct *A* or *D* answer.

____ TOTAL SCORE: Using Words Precisely

• *Enter the total score for each exercise in the spaces below. Then add the scores together to find your Critical Reading Score. Record your Critical Reading Score on the graph on page 114.*

_____	Finding the Main Idea
_____	Recalling Facts
_____	Making Inferences
_____	Using Words Precisely
_____	**CRITICAL READING SCORE: Unit 7**

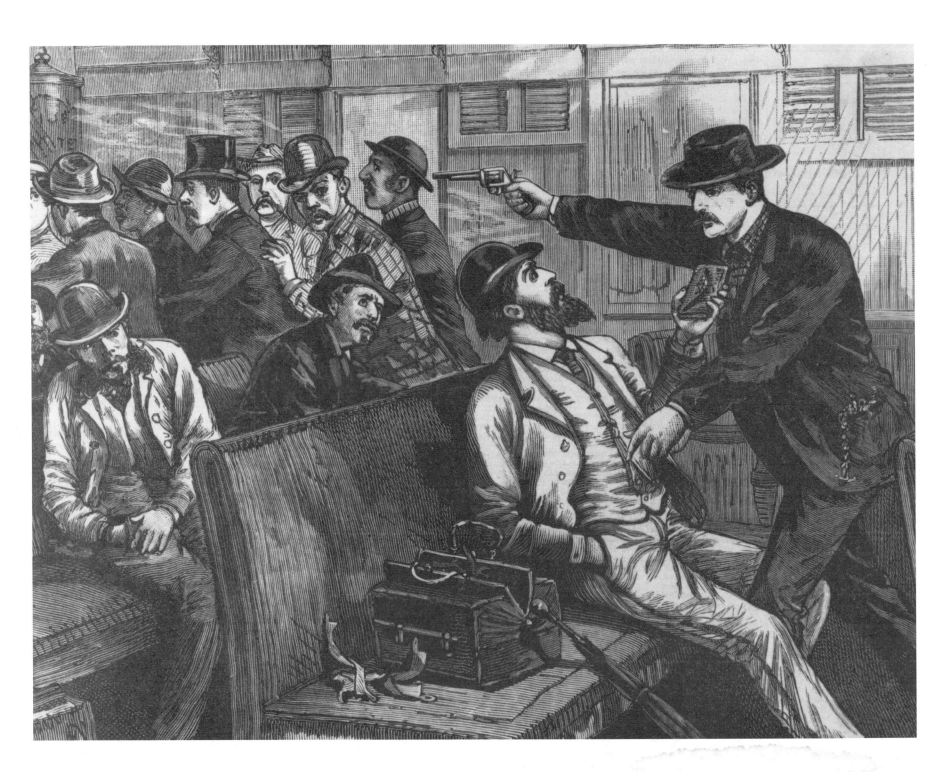

THE GREAT TRAIN ROBBERY

Early in the morning on August 8, 1963, twelve men got ready to pull off the greatest train robbery of all time. They slipped on their gloves and masks. Each thief had a particular job to do. Two broke into a railroad worker's shack. They grabbed some pickaxes as well as a huge crowbar. Another man shinnied up a nearby telephone pole and cut the wires. Three gang members set up a phony red signal light beside the train tracks. According to one of the thieves, everything was "sweet." Now all they had to do was wait.

Soon the mail train from Glasgow, Scotland, would come by. Every day the train passed here on its way to London, England. It had twelve cars plus the engine. The last ten cars carried regular mail, but the second car behind the engine carried something else. It contained special mail sacks, stuffed with small bills. Five postal workers guarded this money.

Just before 3 A.M., the robbers got into position. They waited anxiously along the banks of the railroad tracks. Then Bruce Reynolds, one of the thieves, saw the lights of the mail train in the distance. He picked up his walkie-talkie and said, "It's coming. This is the real thing."

Engineer Jack Mills stood at the controls in the train engine's cab. When he noticed the red light, he slowed the train to a stop. David Whitby, his fireman, climbed out of the engine and walked briskly down the tracks to a telephone box. He wanted to contact the control tower to see if anything was wrong. As he lifted the telephone receiver, he saw that the cord had been cut. Then he looked around. He saw a man in a mask. "What's up, mate?" Whitby asked.

The masked man, named Buster Edwards, motioned to him to come closer. Whitby obeyed. When he got close enough, Edwards threw him down the side of the bank. "Hold him," Edwards shouted to the two men waiting below. As they held Whitby down, one of the men snarled, "If you shout, I'll kill you."

Whitby took the hint. "All right, mate," he said softly.

Next, two of the thieves unhooked the last ten mail cars. The gang wanted to pull the money car away from the rest of the train before they robbed it. That way they wouldn't have to deal with the seventy-one postal clerks sorting the mail in those cars. And in fact, the clerks never suspected a thing. Throughout the entire robbery, they went on calmly sorting the mail.

Meanwhile, Mills was waiting in the engine. He wasn't worried. He figured the delay was caused by some routine problem. After all, a mail train had been running this route for more than a hundred years. No one had ever attempted a robbery along it.

But there's a first time for everything, Mills discovered. Suddenly, three men climbed into

The phrase train robbery *may bring to mind this scene: daring robbers board a train, demand money at gunpoint, and terrify everyone. In the greatest train robbery of all, however, only seven people on the train even knew it was being robbed of over $7,000,000.*

his cab and began beating him with clubs. One of the robbers was a train engineer. He tried to restart the engine but, for some reason, couldn't. So another one of the thieves grabbed the bleeding and badly shaken Mills. He wiped the blood from Mills's face. "Move this train," he shouted with a club in his hand, "or else!"

"All right," said Mills.

Mills restarted the engine and it lurched forward. The last ten cars, uncoupled from the rest, were left behind as the train moved three quarters of a mile down the track. When it reached Bridego Bridge, the thieves ordered Mills to stop. Below the bridge was a road. There the thieves had vehicles waiting for their escape. Using pickaxes and a crowbar, they broke into the money car. The five postal clerks didn't resist.

Working fast, the thieves formed a chain from the train to their vehicles. They tossed the money bags from one man to the next. In just fifteen minutes, they loaded 120 bags. That was two tons of cold cash! The exact amount was later shown to be $7,368,715. Then, at exactly 3:45 A.M., Bruce Reynolds raised his hand. "That's enough," he said. There were still six bags to go. But it wasn't worth the risk. Another train was due. So the thieves left the rest of the bags and took off.

They drove to a nearby farmhouse to divide the loot. Then the group split up. Some of the gang members went to London or other cities to wait until the heat died down. The rest stayed at the farm. But those who stayed had strict instructions. They were supposed to leave the farm within two weeks. They had to burn the money bags and bury the ashes. In addition, they had to wipe the farmhouse clean of all fingerprints. This was absolutely essential. Most of the gang members had been in jail before, so police had their fingerprints on file.

The police started a nationwide manhunt. At first, they came up empty. The robbery had been carefully planned. The thieves hadn't left a trail. But then the police got a lucky break. An army colonel who had nothing to do with the case circled his airplane over the farm. This was a signal to his friends nearby that he intended to pay them a visit. But the robbers thought it was a police plane. They panicked and fled. In their haste, they neglected to burn the money bags. They also forgot to wipe away their fingerprints.

Soon after that, someone called the police about activity at the farm. A neighbor had seen strange men moving about. He also noticed that some of the farm windows had been blackened. When police investigated, they realized they had found the robbers' hideout.

The police rounded up the thieves one by one. It took a few years, but they caught all of them. Most received long prison terms. Still, the police could not claim a total victory. Most of the stolen money was never found. Police believe that much of it is still out there, buried somewhere, waiting to be found.

If you have been timed while reading this selection, enter your reading time below. Then turn to the Words-per-Minute table on page 111 and look up your reading speed (words per minute). Enter your reading speed on the graph on page 113.

READING TIME: Unit 8
_____ : _____
Minutes   *Seconds*

How Well Did You Read?

- *Complete the four exercises that follow. The directions for each exercise will tell you how to mark your answers.*

- *When you have finished all four exercises, use the answer key on page 107 to check your work. For each right answer, put a check mark (✓) on the line beside the box. For each wrong answer, write the correct answer on the line.*

- *Follow the directions after each exercise to find your scores.*

A FINDING THE MAIN IDEA

A good main idea statement answers two questions: it tells *who* or *what* is the subject of the story, and it answers the understood question *does what?* or *is what?* Look at the three statements below. One expresses the main idea of the story you just read. Another statement is *too broad*; it is vague and doesn't tell much about the topic of the story. The third statement is *too narrow*; it tells about only one part of the story.

Match the statements with the three answer choices below by writing the letter of each answer in the box in front of the statement it goes with.

M—Main Idea   B—Too Broad   N—Too Narrow

_____ ☐ 1. Twelve men were in the gang that committed the greatest train robbery to date, the 1963 robbery of a British mail train.

_____ ☐ 2. A well-organized 1963 robbery of a British mail train brought robbers more than $7 million, but the robbers were soon caught.

_____ ☐ 3. Not all train robbers were outlaws in the American West; some of the most daring have been bandits in Britain.

_____ Score 15 points for a correct *M* answer.
_____ Score 5 points for each correct *B* or *N* answer.

_____ TOTAL SCORE: Finding the Main Idea

B RECALLING FACTS

How well do you remember the facts in the story you just read? Put an *x* in the box in front of the correct answer to each of the multiple-choice questions below.

1. The mail train that was robbed was on its way
   - ☐ a. to London, England.
   - ☐ b. to Glasgow, Scotland.
   - ☐ c. through the Chunnel between England and France.

2. All the mail sacks stuffed with money were
   - ☐ a. hidden in the engine cab.
   - ☐ b. in the first mail car behind the engine.
   - ☐ c. in the second mail car behind the engine.

3. The robbers got the train to stop by
   - ☐ a. placing logs on the tracks to cause a wreck.
   - ☐ b. standing next to the tracks and waving.
   - ☐ c. setting up a phony signal light along the tracks.

4. The thieves took
   - ☐ a. all the mail sacks on the train, plus hostages.
   - ☐ b. all but six mail sacks in the second train car.
   - ☐ c. every mail sack in the first train car.

5. The robbers hiding at a farmhouse panicked when
   - ☐ a. a private airplane circled overhead.
   - ☐ b. a police plane circled overhead.
   - ☐ c. neighbors saw strange activity at the farm.

Score 5 points for each correct answer.

_____ TOTAL SCORE: Recalling Facts

C MAKING INFERENCES

When you use information from the text and your own experience to draw a conclusion that is not directly stated in the text, you are making an *inference*.

Below are five statements that may or may *not* be inferences based on the facts of the story. Write the letter *C* in the box in front of each statement that is a correct inference. Write the letter *F* in front of each faulty inference.

C—Correct Inference   F—Faulty Inference

1. The gang in Britain's great train robbery was familiar with the mail train's usual operation.

2. The gang included convicted murderers as well as experienced thieves.

3. The train crew knew that the amount of money carried on this run was much greater than usual.

4. Although the robbers had planned carefully and acted boldly, not all of them were confident of success.

5. The man who planned this crime would have done better to use beginners with no record or experience in robbery.

Score 5 points for each correct *C* or *F* answer.

_____ TOTAL SCORE: Making Inferences

D USING WORDS PRECISELY

Each numbered sentence below contains an underlined word or phrase from the story you have just read. Following the sentence are three definitions. One is a *synonym* for the underlined word, one is an *antonym*, and one has a completely *different* meaning than the underlined word.

For each definition, write the letter that stands for the correct answer in the box.

S—Synonym   A—Antonym   D—Different

1. They waited <u>anxiously</u> along the banks of the railroad tracks.

____ ☐ a. rudely

____ ☐ b. in a cool, unconcerned manner

____ ☐ c. nervously

2. David Whitby, his fireman, climbed out of the engine and walked <u>briskly</u> down the tracks to a telephone box.

____ ☐ a. quickly

____ ☐ b. noiselessly

____ ☐ c. slowly

3. As they held Whitby down, one of the men <u>snarled</u>, "If you shout, I'll kill you."

____ ☐ a. said in a friendly tone

____ ☐ b. wrote

____ ☐ c. growled

4. Some of the gang members went to London or other cities to wait until the <u>heat</u> died down.

____ ☐ a. disease

____ ☐ b. pressure

____ ☐ c. lack of interest, neglect

5. In addition, they had to wipe the farmhouse clean of all fingerprints. This was absolutely <u>essential</u>.

____ ☐ a. unnecessary

____ ☐ b. required

____ ☐ c. boring

____ Score 3 points for a correct *S* answer
____ Score 1 point for each correct *A* or *D* answer

____ TOTAL SCORE: Using Words Precisely

• *Enter the total score for each exercise in the spaces below. Then add the scores together to find your Critical Reading Score. Record your Critical Reading Score on the graph on page 114.*

_____ Finding the Main Idea
_____ Recalling Facts
_____ Making Inferences
_____ Using Words Precisely

_____ CRITICAL READING SCORE: Unit 8

Even crooks need a break now and then. John Dillinger thought so when he took a girlfriend to the movies at this theater in Chicago. He didn't know she had tipped off FBI agents, who waited for him outside.

JOHN DILLINGER: A CROOK WITH STYLE

John Dillinger could have done anything he wanted with his life. He was a smart kid with a lot of friends. He had plenty of courage. And he was a terrific athlete. In fact, the governor of Indiana once declared, "That kid ought to be playing major league baseball." But John Dillinger did not become a baseball player or a businessman or a teacher. He became a criminal.

Dillinger was born in Indianapolis in 1903. By the time he got to sixth grade, he was already breaking the law. He stole coal from a railroad yard. Then he sold it to neighbors as heating fuel for their homes.

Dillinger got into real trouble when he was twenty-one. He tried to rob an elderly store owner. No one was hurt in the robbery, but Dillinger wound up in police hands. The police encouraged him to plead guilty. They assured him that if he did, the judge would go easy on him. Dillinger took their advice and pleaded guilty. But the judge was in a bad mood that day. He slapped Dillinger with a sentence of ten to twenty years.

The harsh punishment shocked everyone. The store owner himself later asked that the sentence be cut down. Even so, Dillinger served nine years in prison. By the time he got out, he was filled with contempt for the law. Still, from his point of view, the years in prison had not been a total loss. He had become friends with some other convicts. They had taught him everything they knew about robbing banks. When Dillinger was released, he promised not to forget them. He vowed to return and help them escape as soon as he could.

First, though, Dillinger needed some cash. So, in the summer of 1933, he robbed a string of banks. Dillinger planned his crimes with great care. He studied the alarm system of each bank. He laid out escape routes and picked good hideouts. But what really set Dillinger apart from other robbers was the style he brought to the job. He would stroll into a bank dressed in a nice suit. Pulling out his gun, he would politely ask the tellers to hand over the money. Often he would leap over a railing or two, moving with an easy grace that impressed everyone. Sometimes he would even flirt with women in the bank. Word of his actions spread quickly. More and more people began to talk about this dashing bank robber named John Dillinger.

By September, Dillinger had quite a stash of money. True to his word, he remembered his friends back in prison. He arranged to have weapons smuggled in to them. Armed with those weapons, ten of Dillinger's buddies broke free.

Over the next twelve months, Dillinger and this gang of thieves tore across the country. They robbed bank after bank. Sometimes they got just a few thousand dollars. But often they made off with much more. On October 23, 1933, they walked away with more than $75,000. It was Dillinger's biggest haul. It was also the robbery that made him a folk hero in the eyes of many people. Again, it wasn't just what he did—it was the way he did it.

On that October day, Dillinger and his men went to Greencastle, Indiana. They entered the Central National Bank. With a gun in his hand, Dillinger made a dramatic leap over a railing. He and his men then stuffed fistfuls of money into their sacks. As they were leaving, Dillinger noticed a man off to the side. He was a farmer who had come to put some money in the bank. His money still lay on the counter in front of a teller's window.

Dillinger looked at the stack of bills. "Is that your money or the bank's?" he asked.

"Mine," said the farmer.

"Keep it," Dillinger told him. "We only want the bank's."

It was that kind of remark that made Dillinger famous. Sure, he was a crook, people said. But he was such an *honorable* crook! The police took a different view. They knew Dillinger and his gang had killed several people. The thieves shot anyone who got in their way. More victims could fall any day. So the police put Dillinger on their Most Wanted list.

Actually, the police got their hands on Dillinger a couple of times. But both times he broke out of jail before a trial could be held. His most spectacular escape came on March 3, 1934. Dillinger had been put in jail in Crown Point, Indiana. Everyone said that jail was escape-proof. Dozens of extra guards were brought in just to make sure of that. Somehow, though, John Dillinger got his hands on a weapon. It is not clear whether he used a real gun or simply a piece of wood shaped like a gun. In any case, it looked real enough to the guards. Dillinger flashed it at them, then escaped down a flight of stairs.

By July 1934, Dillinger's gang had stolen more than $250,000. And they had done it in just a few months. But Dillinger's days as a high-flying gangster were coming to an end. According to police, he was betrayed by one of his girlfriends. Anna Sage came to the Chicago police. She offered to take them to Dillinger. In return, they agreed to help her get out of some legal troubles.

Police records show that on July 22, Sage went to a movie with Dillinger. She wore a red dress so police agents could spot her in the crowd. When she walked out of the theater with Dillinger, six agents moved in. Sensing trouble, Dillinger whirled and reached for his gun. But the agents were ready. Three of them fired at Dillinger, who dropped to the ground, dead.

That is one version of the story. But another version says that it was not John Dillinger who died outside a Chicago theater that day. According to this story, Anna Sage tricked police. She had told them that she would be with Dillinger. However, some people claim, her unfortunate companion was really a small-time crook named Jimmy Lawrence.

There are a few facts to support this theory. Doctors who examined the body said the dead man had a damaged heart. Dillinger could not have made his fancy leaps with such a heart. He could never have played baseball, either. Doctors said they found no scars on the dead man. But Dillinger's body should have shown a couple of old bullet wounds. Finally, doctors said the dead man's eyes were brown. Dillinger's were blue.

It may be that the doctors were sloppy when they examined Dillinger's body. Or it may be that police shot the wrong man. We'll never know for sure. All we know is this: after July 22, 1934, John Dillinger never bothered anyone again.

If you have been timed while reading this selection, enter your reading time below. Then turn to the Words-per-Minute table on page 111 and look up your reading speed (words per minute). Enter your reading speed on the graph on page 113.

READING TIME: Unit 9
_____ : _____
Minutes   Seconds

How Well Did You Read?

- *Complete the four exercises that follow. The directions for each exercise will tell you how to mark your answers.*

- *When you have finished all four exercises, use the answer key on page 107 to check your work. For each right answer, put a check mark (✓) on the line beside the box. For each wrong answer, write the correct answer on the line.*

- *Follow the directions after each exercise to find your scores.*

 A FINDING THE MAIN IDEA

A good main idea statement answers two questions: it tells *who* or *what* is the subject of the story, and it answers the understood question *does what?* or *is what?* Look at the three statements below. One expresses the main idea of the story you just read. Another statement is *too broad*; it is vague and doesn't tell much about the topic of the story. The third statement is *too narrow*; it tells about only one part of the story.

Match the statements with the three answer choices below by writing the letter of each answer in the box in front of the statement it goes with.

M—Main Idea   B—Too Broad   N—Too Narrow

____ ☐ 1. During the 1930s, several criminals caught the attention of the American public.

____ ☐ 2. In his short career in crime, bank robber John Dillinger impressed the public with his daring and style.

____ ☐ 3. According to some sources, John Dillinger once escaped from jail using only a piece of wood shaped like a gun.

____ Score 15 points for a correct *M* answer.
____ Score 5 points for each correct *B* or *N* answer.

____ TOTAL SCORE: Finding the Main Idea

B RECALLING FACTS

How well do you remember the facts in the story you just read? Put an *x* in the box in front of the correct answer to each of the multiple-choice questions below.

1. John Dillinger first went to jail for
   - ☐ a. killing a bank guard.
   - ☐ b. stealing a car.
   - ☐ c. robbing an elderly store owner.

2. While in jail, Dillinger
   - ☐ a. finished high school.
   - ☐ b. learned about robbing banks from other convicts.
   - ☐ c. had time to plan his escape.

3. In Dillinger's single biggest bank robbery, he stole
   - ☐ a. less than $10,000.
   - ☐ b. more than $75,000.
   - ☐ c. about $1 million.

4. To make sure Dillinger wouldn't escape from the jail at Crown Point, Indiana, officials
   - ☐ a. built a special fence.
   - ☐ b. put Dillinger in a cell in the basement.
   - ☐ c. brought in dozens of extra guards.

5. Police finally gunned down Dillinger as he
   - ☐ a. left a movie theater.
   - ☐ b. escaped from jail.
   - ☐ c. robbed another bank.

Score 5 points for each correct answer.

_____ TOTAL SCORE: Recalling Facts

C MAKING INFERENCES

When you use information from the text and your own experience to draw a conclusion that is not directly stated in the text, you are making an *inference*.

Below are five statements that may or may *not* be inferences based on the facts of the story. Write the letter *C* in the box in front of each statement that is a correct inference. Write the letter *F* in front of each faulty inference.

C—Correct Inference   F—Faulty Inference

1. Dillinger might have led a normal life if he had not been given such a harsh sentence for his first crime.

2. John Dillinger was an impatient man who could not be bothered with details.

3. Dillinger was honest in his dealings with his friends.

4. During the 1930s, newspapers and radio broadcasts never described the details of robberies.

5. John Dillinger sometimes wore a gun in public even when he was not planning on using it.

Score 5 points for each correct *C* or *F* answer.

_____ TOTAL SCORE: Making Inferences

D USING WORDS PRECISELY

Each numbered sentence below contains an underlined word or phrase from the story you have just read. Following the sentence are three definitions. One is a *synonym* for the underlined word, one is an *antonym*, and one has a completely *different* meaning than the underlined word.

For each definition, write the letter that stands for the correct answer in the box.

S—Synonym   A—Antonym   D—Different

1. By the time he got out, he was filled with <u>contempt</u> for the law.

____ ☐ a. respect

____ ☐ b. scorn

____ ☐ c. questions

2. When Dillinger was <u>released</u>, he promised not to forget them.

____ ☐ a. set free

____ ☐ b. older

____ ☐ c. imprisoned

3. But he was such an <u>*honorable*</u> crook!

____ ☐ a. shameful

____ ☐ b. handsome

____ ☐ c. worthy of respect

4. More and more people began to talk about this <u>dashing</u> bank robber named John Dillinger.

____ ☐ a. stylish, showy

____ ☐ b. dull

____ ☐ c. balding

5. His most <u>spectacular</u> escape came on March 3, 1934.

____ ☐ a. comfortable

____ ☐ b. ordinary

____ ☐ c. stunning

____ Score 3 points for a correct *S* answer.
____ Score 1 point for each correct *A* or *D* answer.

____ TOTAL SCORE: Using Words Precisely

• *Enter the total score for each exercise in the spaces below. Then add the scores together to find your Critical Reading Score. Record your Critical Reading Score on the graph on page 114.*

_____	Finding the Main Idea
_____	Recalling Facts
_____	Making Inferences
_____	Using Words Precisely
_____	CRITICAL READING SCORE: Unit 9

ASSASSIN!

On April 4, 1968, Dr. Martin Luther King, Jr., went to Memphis, Tennessee. He checked into the Lorraine Motel. Early that evening, he strolled out onto the balcony. Some friends joined him there. Suddenly, from the shadows, someone fired a single rifle blast. A bullet smashed into Dr. King's neck. The bullet's force was so great that it ripped the necktie right off him. Within an hour, Dr. King was dead. The death of this great African American leader shocked the nation. Police quickly began a massive search for the assassin.

The police figured out that the fatal shot had come from a nearby rooming house. The assassin had been sloppy. He had left his rifle near the scene. The police were able to get a clear fingerprint off this weapon. They traced the print to a small-time crook named James Earl Ray.

James Earl Ray? Just the thought of

Grouped around Dr. Martin Luther King's body, his friends point to the source of the rifle shot that felled him. But the assassin has already fled.

Ray as an assassin baffled the police. What reason did he have to shoot Dr. King? He was not a known racist or King hater. In fact, James Earl Ray had never seemed like much of a threat to anyone. He had dropped out of high school after tenth grade. He had tried army life, but with no success. Eventually, he had turned to a life of crime.

But Ray had not been very good at that, either. He once dropped his wallet during a robbery. That made it easy for police to prove he was the thief. Another time he was caught after falling out of a getaway car. His only "success" came in 1967. That year, he broke out of the Missouri State Prison. Even then, police were not exactly terrified. They put a puny $50 reward out for his capture.

And yet, *his* fingerprint was on the gun that killed Dr. King. So the police went looking for Ray. This time they set the reward at $100,000. But for the first time ever, they had trouble catching him. The man who had botched most of his other crimes now acted like a real professional criminal.

First, he fled to Toronto. There he

obtained a Canadian passport. In those days, that was easy to do. Ray simply paid $8 and swore that he was a Canadian citizen. The name he used was Ramon Sneyd.

Ray stayed in Canada for about a month. Then, on May 5, he used his phony passport to fly to England. He arrived in London on May 6. Soon after that, he flew to Portugal for five days. The reason for these trips has never been clear. Some people think Ray was just trying to elude police. Others think he was meeting someone who paid him to assassinate Dr. King. No one knows for sure.

Meanwhile, U.S. agents had picked up Ray's trail. They, too, knew how easy it was to get a Canadian passport. So they asked the police in Canada to sift through 300,000 passport applications. At last, one officer found Ray's photo on a form for Ramon Sneyd. Suddenly the manhunt heated up.

Back in England, Ray bounced from one cheap hotel to another. He must have known that the police were closing in. Using the name Sneyd, he called several newspapers. He asked how he could join some white army group in Africa. Ray must have thought he would be safe there. "Foreign legions" were famous for not asking about a person's history. One newspaper reporter suggested that Ray go to Belgium. Some white army groups were recruiting new soldiers there.

By now, however, the net had closed in on Ray. On June 8, "Sneyd" went to the airport. Just as he was about to board his plane to Belgium, the English police arrested him. They sent Ray back to the United States. He pleaded guilty and was sentenced to ninety-nine years in prison. The day after he was sentenced, Ray changed his story. He tried to take back his plea, claiming that he had been forced to plead guilty. But it was too late. No one was listening.

For many people, the sentencing of James Earl Ray ended the story. But for others, questions remain. The most important one is this: Did Ray act alone? Agents for the U.S. government have always maintained that he did. But other people disagree. In 1978, a special panel studied the case. Panel members found a "likelihood" that other people were involved. James Earl Ray's own father said, "[James] couldn't have planned it alone. He wasn't smart enough for that."

If Ray did not act alone, then who helped him? Who told him what to do? Who planned—and paid for—his escape? No one knows. Some believe that a group of racists masterminded the killing. Others think U.S. leaders were behind the plot. According to this theory, the leaders did not like Dr. King. They did not like the way he stirred up the African American community.

If Ray did take directions from someone, why did he do it? What could have persuaded him to kill Dr. King? Many think his motive was simple. He wanted money. All the other crimes he had committed had been for money. According to one rumor, Ray was paid $50,000 for the murder. But like the other theories, this one has never been proven.

Many years have now passed since the assassination. The whole truth about it may never be known. But one fact remains. No one else has been charged in the murder of Dr. King. James Earl Ray is still the only one serving time for the assassination.

If you have been timed while reading this selection, enter your reading time below. Then turn to the Words-per-Minute table on page 111 and look up your reading speed (words per minute). Enter your reading speed on the graph on page 113.

READING TIME: Unit 10

_____ : _____

Minutes   *Seconds*

How Well Did You Read?

- *Complete the four exercises that follow. The directions for each exercise will tell you how to mark your answers.*

- *When you have finished all four exercises, use the answer key on page 107 to check your work. For each right answer, put a check mark (✓) on the line beside the box. For each wrong answer, write the correct answer on the line.*

- *Follow the directions after each exercise to find your scores.*

A FINDING THE MAIN IDEA

A good main idea statement answers two questions: it tells *who* or *what* is the subject of the story, and it answers the understood question *does what?* or *is what?* Look at the three statements below. One expresses the main idea of the story you just read. Another statement is *too broad*; it is vague and doesn't tell much about the topic of the story. The third statement is *too narrow*; it tells about only one part of the story.

Match the statements with the three answer choices below by writing the letter of each answer in the box in front of the statement it goes with.

M—Main Idea   B—Too Broad   N—Too Narrow

____ ☐ 1. Details about the assassination of Martin Luther King, Jr., by James Earl Ray remain a mystery today.

____ ☐ 2. Certain crimes fascinate and puzzle people long after the court decision has been made.

____ ☐ 3. James Earl Ray was able to get a Canadian passport just by swearing that he was a Canadian citizen.

____ Score 15 points for a correct *M* answer.
____ Score 5 points for each correct *B* or *N* answer.

____ TOTAL SCORE: Finding the Main Idea

B RECALLING FACTS

How well do you remember the facts in the story you just read? Put an *x* in the box in front of the correct answer to each of the multiple-choice questions below.

1. Dr. King was killed by a blast from a
   - ___ ☐ a. rifle.
   - ___ ☐ b. handgun.
   - ___ ☐ c. machine gun.

2. James Earl Ray's education had ended after
   - ___ ☐ a. the eighth grade.
   - ___ ☐ b. one year of college.
   - ___ ☐ c. the tenth grade.

3. Police went after James Earl Ray because
   - ___ ☐ a. they knew he was a racist and a King hater.
   - ___ ☐ b. his fingerprints were on the weapon they had found.
   - ___ ☐ c. he looked guilty and ran away.

4. Ray first fled to Canada, then to
   - ___ ☐ a. England.
   - ___ ☐ b. France.
   - ___ ☐ c. Portugal.

5. English police arrested Ray just as he was about to
   - ___ ☐ a. assassinate the prime minister of England.
   - ___ ☐ b. go back into his hotel in London.
   - ___ ☐ c. board a plane for Belgium.

Score 5 points for each correct answer.

___ TOTAL SCORE: Recalling Facts

C MAKING INFERENCES

When you use information from the text and your own experience to draw a conclusion that is not directly stated in the text, you are making an *inference*.

Below are five statements that may or may *not* be inferences based on the facts of the story. Write the letter *C* in the box in front of each statement that is a correct inference. Write the letter *F* in front of each faulty inference.

C—Correct Inference   F—Faulty Inference

- ___ ☐ 1. Police were not very interested in finding the assassin of Martin Luther King, Jr.

- ___ ☐ 2. The police had probably kept their eyes on James Earl Ray even before the assassination because they expected him to try to kill Dr. King.

- ___ ☐ 3. U.S. agents felt that they could count on help from the Canadian police.

- ___ ☐ 4. James Earl Ray felt safe and comfortable during his stay in England.

- ___ ☐ 5. To get a Canadian passport in 1968, you needed a photograph of yourself.

Score 5 points for each correct *C* or *F* answer.

___ TOTAL SCORE: Making Inferences

D USING WORDS PRECISELY

Each numbered sentence below contains an underlined word or phrase from the story you have just read. Following the sentence are three definitions. One is a *synonym* for the underlined word, one is an *antonym*, and one has a completely *different* meaning than the underlined word.

For each definition, write the letter that stands for the correct answer in the box.

S—Synonym   A—Antonym   D—Different

1. They put a <u>puny</u> $50 reward out for his capture.

____ ☐ a. generous

____ ☐ b. very small

____ ☐ c. puzzling

2. The man who had <u>botched</u> most of his other crimes now acted like a real, professional criminal.

____ ☐ a. ruined

____ ☐ b. planned

____ ☐ c. successfully performed

3. "<u>Foreign</u> legions" were famous for not asking about a person's history.

____ ☐ a. having to do with laws

____ ☐ b. having to do with your own country

____ ☐ c. having to do with another country

4. Some people think that Ray was just trying to <u>elude</u> police.

____ ☐ a. dodge

____ ☐ b. seek out

____ ☐ c. help

5. Agents for the U.S. government have always <u>maintained</u> that he did.

____ ☐ a. recalled

____ ☐ b. declared to be true

____ ☐ c. denied

____ Score 3 points for a correct *S* answer.
____ Score 1 point for each correct *A* or *D* answer.

____ TOTAL SCORE: Using Words Precisely

• *Enter the total score for each exercise in the spaces below. Then add the scores together to find your Critical Reading Score. Record your Critical Reading Score on the graph on page 114.*

_____ Finding the Main Idea
_____ Recalling Facts
_____ Making Inferences
_____ Using Words Precisely

_____ CRITICAL READING SCORE: Unit 10

Group Three

Does this smiling convict look like Public Enemy #1? George Kelly, an easygoing petty thief, got into real trouble when he kidnapped a rich oilman. Both Machine Gun Kelly and his wife, Kathryn, were given life sentences for the crime Kathryn had masterminded.

MACHINE GUN KELLY: PUBLIC ENEMY NUMBER ONE

The police called him Public Enemy Number One. His wife, Kathryn, nicknamed him Machine Gun Kelly. To be sure, George R. Kelly was a criminal. There is no doubt about that. And he certainly talked like a real tough guy. Kelly liked to brag that "no copper [police officer] will ever take me alive." But was he all that bad? Was he the terror that the press made him out to be? Or was Kelly just an easygoing thief who happened to marry the wrong woman?

Kelly began his life of crime as a bootlegger during the 1920s. (A bootlegger is someone who sells illegal liquor.) But he wasn't very good at it. The police usually caught him. They either kicked him out of town or gave him a few months in jail. As one person put it, Kelly was "a good-natured slob, a bootlegger who spilled more [liquor] than he delivered."

That changed in 1927, the year Kelly met Kathryn Shannon. Before their fateful meeting, Kelly didn't even like guns. And he never hurt anyone. But Kathryn was an ambitious and ruthless woman. She soon saw that despite all the tough talk, George Kelly was really just a marshmallow. "You've got to be able to hurt people," she told him. "You've got to be tough or nobody will respect you."

Kathryn and Kelly were married, and she set out to toughen him up. She gave him a machine gun. She made him practice shooting walnuts off fence posts. In time, he became good enough to write his name on a wall with bullets. Kathryn also made sure that Kelly's reputation grew. She dreamed up phony stories about the big banks Kelly robbed. Kathryn even gave away empty bullet shells saying, "Have a souvenir of my husband, Machine Gun Kelly."

By 1931 Kelly had moved up the criminal ladder. The former bootlegger began to rob real banks. But he picked small country banks without much money. That was not good enough for Kathryn. She wanted to do something big. She had read stories about kidnappers getting huge ransoms. She began nagging Kelly to kidnap someone with lots of money. It was the only way to get rich, she insisted.

"Too risky," Kelly told her. But she kept pushing. Finally—as usual—

Machine Gun Kelly gave in. He joined up with Albert Bates, another petty crook. They agreed to kidnap a rich Oklahoma City oilman named Charles Urschel.

On the night of July 22, 1933, Kelly and Bates broke into Urschel's home. They found the oilman and his wife playing cards with another couple. That confused Kelly. He was so incompetent that he hadn't bothered to find out what Urschel looked like. "Which one's Urschel?" he barked.

Neither man answered. "All right," Kelly said at last, "we'll take both of you."

Kelly and Bates drove off with the two men. After a while, Kelly thought to look in their wallets. Only then did he discover who the real Urschel was. He and Bates kicked the other man out of the car, then continued on with the blindfolded Urschel.

They took the oilman to a ranch owned by Kathryn's parents in Paradise, Texas. From there, the Kellys demanded a ransom of $200,000. The Urschel family agreed to pay. But with Machine Gun Kelly in charge, collecting the money wasn't easy.

Kelly missed one meeting because he couldn't get his car started. Finally, after eight days, he collected the ransom.

Kathryn now wanted to kill Urschel. For once in his life, Kelly stood up to her. He convinced Bates and Kathryn to let Urschel go. Kelly pointed out that shooting him would "be bad for future business."

All this time, Charles Urschel had been alert and listening. The oilman had a keen memory. He noticed many details about his kidnapping. He hoped the police could later use these details to catch his captors. Urschel noted that the car ride had taken about twelve hours over bumpy roads. He also noticed that a plane passed overhead twice a day. He even figured out the times—9:15 A.M. and 5:45 P.M.

After his release, Urschel gave these facts to agents from the Federal Bureau of Investigation. They knew what the twelve-hour ride over bumpy roads meant. It meant the ranch was within three hundred miles of Oklahoma City. The agents also studied hundreds of flight plans. They found the spot where daily flights crossed at 9:15 A.M and 5:45 P.M. That spot was Paradise.

The FBI was now hot on the trail of Machine Gun Kelly. Agents labeled him Public Enemy Number One. Kelly and his wife ran, but they couldn't hide. Investigators tracked them down at a cheap hotel in Memphis, Tennessee. Three police officers burst into Kelly's room. One shoved a shotgun into Kelly's stomach. Poor old Machine Gun gave up without a fight. "I've been waiting for you all night," he said softly.

At their trial, Kathryn turned against her husband. She tried to put all the blame on him. No one listened. Machine Gun, Kathryn, and Bates all got life sentences. It was a pitiful end for this so-called tough guy. Prison life at Leavenworth and Alcatraz was hard on George Machine Gun Kelly. His fellow inmates often laughed at him. They even gave him a new nickname—Pop Gun Kelly.

Just before he died in 1954, Kelly wrote a letter to his old victim, Charles Urschel. "These five words seem written in fire on the walls of my cell," Kelly wrote. "Nothing can be worth this!" He might have said the same thing about his marriage to Kathryn.

If you have been timed while reading this selection, enter your reading time below. Then turn to the Words-per-Minute table on page 112 and look up your reading speed (words per minute). Enter your reading speed on the graph on page 113.

READING TIME: Unit 11
_____ : _____
Minutes   *Seconds*

How Well Did You Read?

- *Complete the four exercises that follow. The directions for each exercise will tell you how to mark your answers.*

- *When you have finished all four exercises, use the answer key on page 108 to check your work. For each right answer, put a check mark (✓) on the line beside the box. For each wrong answer, write the correct answer on the line.*

- *Follow the directions after each exercise to find your scores.*

A FINDING THE MAIN IDEA

A good main idea statement answers two questions: it tells *who* or *what* is the subject of the story, and it answers the understood question *does what?* or *is what?* Look at the three statements below. One expresses the main idea of the story you just read. Another statement is *too broad*; it is vague and doesn't tell much about the topic of the story. The third statement is *too narrow*; it tells about only one part of the story.

Match the statements with the three answer choices below by writing the letter of each answer in the box in front of the statement it goes with.

M—Main Idea   B—Too Broad   N—Too Narrow

_____ ☐ 1. The FBI considered Machine Gun Kelly to be a dangerous criminal.

_____ ☐ 2. When Machine Gun Kelly broke into Charles Urschel's house to kidnap him, he couldn't recognize Urschel.

_____ ☐ 3. Machine Gun Kelly, encouraged by his wife, Kathryn, became a famous robber and kidnapper during the 1930s.

_____ Score 15 points for a correct *M* answer.
_____ Score 5 points for each correct *B* or *N* answer.

_____ TOTAL SCORE: Finding the Main Idea

B RECALLING FACTS

How well do you remember the facts in the story you just read? Put an *x* in the box in front of the correct answer to each of the multiple-choice questions below.

1. George Kelly began his life of crime as a
   - ___ ☐ a. train robber.
   - ___ ☐ b. petty thief.
   - ___ ☐ c. bootlegger.

2. To help George improve his machine gun skills, Kathryn made him practice shooting
   - ___ ☐ a. tin cans thrown into the air.
   - ___ ☐ b. walnuts off fence posts.
   - ___ ☐ c. a target with a big bull's-eye in the center.

3. To get rich, Kathryn urged George to
   - ___ ☐ a. rob a big bank in a major city.
   - ___ ☐ b. threaten to blow up a government building if they weren't given a million dollars.
   - ___ ☐ c. kidnap a rich person and demand a huge ransom.

4. After the $200,000 was paid, Kathryn wanted to
   - ___ ☐ a. kill Mr. Urschel.
   - ___ ☐ b. let Mr. Urschel go immediately.
   - ___ ☐ c. make Mr. Urschel part of the gang.

5. Machine Gun and Kathryn were captured in
   - ___ ☐ a. Memphis, Tennessee.
   - ___ ☐ b. Nashville, Tennessee.
   - ___ ☐ c. Tallahassee, Florida.

Score 5 points for each correct answer.

___ TOTAL SCORE: Recalling Facts

C MAKING INFERENCES

When you use information from the text and your own experience to draw a conclusion that is not directly stated in the text, you are making an *inference*.

Below are five statements that may or may *not* be inferences based on the facts of the story. Write the letter *C* in the box in front of each statement that is a correct inference. Write the letter *F* in front of each faulty inference.

C—Correct Inference   F—Faulty Inference

- ___ ☐ 1. Machine Gun Kelly would probably never have committed any crimes if he hadn't met Kathryn.

- ___ ☐ 2. The crime of bootlegging was considered less serious than the crime of kidnapping.

- ___ ☐ 3. Country banks didn't hold as much money as city banks because most country people were poorer than most city people.

- ___ ☐ 4. Machine Gun Kelly always planned his crimes carefully, with great attention to every detail.

- ___ ☐ 5. Although Machine Gun Kelly was willing to commit many crimes, he did not wish to commit murder.

Score 5 points for each correct *C* or *F* answer.

___ TOTAL SCORE: Making Inferences

D USING WORDS PRECISELY

Each numbered sentence below contains an underlined word or phrase from the story you have just read. Following the sentence are three definitions. One is a *synonym* for the underlined word, one is an *antonym*, and one has a completely *different* meaning than the underlined word.

For each definition, write the letter that stands for the correct answer in the box.

S—Synonym   A—Antonym   D—Different

1. But Kathryn was an <u>ambitious</u> and ruthless woman.

____ ☐ a. popular

____ ☐ b. full of the drive to succeed

____ ☐ c. lazy

2. He hoped the police could later use these details to catch his <u>captors</u>.

____ ☐ a. people who capture others

____ ☐ b. people who set others free

____ ☐ c. people who kill others

3. He joined up with Albert Bates, another <u>petty</u> crook.

____ ☐ a. major

____ ☐ b. cute

____ ☐ c. unimportant

4. He was so <u>incompetent</u> that he hadn't bothered to find out what Urschel looked like.

____ ☐ a. unfit

____ ☐ b. capable

____ ☐ c. surprised

5. The oilman had a <u>keen</u> memory.

____ ☐ a. dull

____ ☐ b. happy

____ ☐ c. sharp

____ Score 3 points for a correct *S* answer.
____ Score 1 point for each correct *A* or *D* answer.

____ TOTAL SCORE: Using Words Precisely

• *Enter the total score for each exercise in the spaces below. Then add the scores together to find your Critical Reading Score. Record your Critical Reading Score on the graph on page 114.*

_____ Finding the Main Idea
_____ Recalling Facts
_____ Making Inferences
_____ Using Words Precisely

_____ CRITICAL READING SCORE: Unit 11

An ID card with this photo might have backed up its owner's claim to being a Serbian army officer . . . a Romanian diplomat . . . a U.S. Army pilot . . . or a prison reform expert. Talented impostor Stephen Jacob Weinberg had the power to convince people he could be and do almost anything.

STEPHEN JACOB WEINBERG: THE MAN WITH MANY FACES

His parents named him Stephen Jacob Weinberg, but he rarely used that name. Weinberg, who was born in Brooklyn in 1890, loved to make up new names for himself. He loved to pretend he was someone with an important job. Often he used the name Stanley Clifford Weyman or something close to it. For nearly forty years, Weinberg played all sorts of make-believe roles. This daring impostor fooled most people. But sooner or later, someone always found out who he really was. Sometimes the police let him off with a warning. Other times he went to jail.

Weinberg was a bright young man. With some hard work, he might have become a doctor or a pilot or a diplomat or a navy officer. But Weinberg had two problems. First, he lacked the patience to go to college and study for any of these professions. Second, he wanted to hold *all* these jobs. He decided there was only one thing to do. He would pretend to be whatever he wanted. That way he could be a doctor one day and something else the next.

Being a good impostor isn't easy.

Weinberg quickly learned how hard it could be. In 1912 he posed as "Clifford Weinberg, the American Consul to Morocco." Earlier, Weinberg had stolen a camera from a photographer's shop. One day the shop owner showed up at a photo session for "Consul" Weinberg. The owner recognized the "consul" as a thief, and Weinberg ended up in jail.

After he got out, Weinberg tried to get honest work. But every job he got seemed dull next to the jobs he dreamed up in his head. So Weinberg went back to his fantasies. He became "Lieutenant Royale St. Cyr," a U.S. Army pilot. He also took on the role of a U.S. Navy officer. For a while, he posed as an army officer from Serbia. He also became "Ethan Allen Weinberg," a diplomat from Romania. Some people said Weinberg looked good in a military uniform. He must have—he certainly wore enough of them! He also wore plenty of prison uniforms. Between 1913 and 1918, he was in and out of jail at least four times.

By 1920 Weinberg was ready for another challenge. A New York company needed a doctor to go to Peru. The doctor would check out health conditions at a work site there. A "Dr. Clifford Wyman" applied for the job. Like all the other applicants, he was interviewed by a real doctor. "Dr. Wyman" completely fooled the interviewer. He made such a good impression that he got the job.

Soon "Dr. Wyman" set sail for Peru. There he rented a fancy house, bought a nice car, and gave huge parties. He had all his bills sent to the company back in New York. The local workers liked "Dr. Wyman" very much. And why not? He simply approved everything they did. But at last, company officials found out who "Dr. Wyman" really was. They fired him but didn't press charges. Perhaps they were too embarrassed about hiring him in the first place!

In 1921 Princess Fatima of Afghanistan arrived in New York. She hoped to meet U.S. President Warren Harding. And she did. The meeting was set up by someone dressed as a navy officer. He said his name was "Sterling Clifford Wyman." No one questioned "Wyman." He seemed to know exactly what he was doing. He even got the princess to pay for all his expenses. (He told her it was an American custom.) She finally smartened up when "Wyman" offered to help her sell her priceless forty-two-carat diamond. Later, the police caught on as well. Weinberg was arrested and charged with impersonating a navy officer. He was sent to prison for two years.

Still, Weinberg refused to quit role-playing. He loved the thrill of it. A little jail time seemed a small price to pay for such grand adventures. Once, Weinberg even tried to pass himself off as a "prison reform expert." There was just one problem. His old prison warden recognized him! Another time, Weinberg started up his own law office. But since he had no license to practice law, that led to another term behind bars.

During World War II, Weinberg began calling himself a "Selective Service consultant." That sounded pretty good. But what Weinberg was doing was illegal. He was teaching young men how to avoid serving in the army. He taught them, for example, how to fake deafness. Again,

he was caught and sent to prison.

Weinberg got out of jail in 1948. He decided to become a reporter. As "Stanley Clifford Weyman," he got a job with the Erwin News Service. His task was to cover the United Nations. Mr. Erwin later said, "Weyman had good news sense—and he seemed to know everybody."

"Weyman" was so good, in fact, that he got his own radio show on WFDR. Every day he gave a five-minute comment on the news. Once a week he had special guests join him on the show. They included top diplomats from all over the world. Some diplomats from Thailand were especially impressed with him. ("Weyman" had convinced them that he had worked as a spy on their behalf during World War II.) In 1951 the Thais offered "Weyman" a job as their own press officer. For Weinberg this was a dream come true. He would now be a real diplomat.

But, as usual, Weinberg was caught. He started wondering how the job would affect him as an American citizen. So he wrote a letter to the State Department asking about it. Officials there checked into

Weinberg's background. It isn't hard to guess the rest of the story. The embarrassed Thais withdrew the job offer. And Weinberg lost his job with the Erwin News Service.

By 1960 Weinberg was an old man. He took a job working as a night clerk in a New York hotel. But he still had dreams of glory. One night two gunmen came in to rob the cash box. Weinberg had no weapon, but he tried to fight off the robbers anyway. The gunmen shot him, then fled without the money. As Weinberg lay dying, perhaps he took some comfort in knowing his last role in life was that of a hero.

If you have been timed while reading this selection, enter your reading time below. Then turn to the Words-per-Minute table on page 112 and look up your reading speed (words per minute). Enter your reading speed on the graph on page 113.

READING TIME: Unit 12
_____ : _____
Minutes   *Seconds*

How Well Did You Read?

- *Complete the four exercises that follow. The directions for each exercise will tell you how to mark your answers.*

- *When you have finished all four exercises, use the answer key on page 108 to check your work. For each right answer, put a check mark (✓) on the line beside the box. For each wrong answer, write the correct answer on the line.*

- *Follow the directions after each exercise to find your scores.*

A FINDING THE MAIN IDEA

A good main idea statement answers two questions: it tells *who* or *what* is the subject of the story, and it answers the understood question *does what?* or *is what?* Look at the three statements below. One expresses the main idea of the story you just read. Another statement is *too broad*; it is vague and doesn't tell much about the topic of the story. The third statement is *too narrow*; it tells about only one part of the story.

Match the statements with the three answer choices below by writing the letter of each answer in the box in front of the statement it goes with.

M—Main Idea   **B—Too Broad**   **N—Too Narrow**

____ ☐ 1. Impersonating other people may be illegal and can land a person in jail.

____ ☐ 2. Stephen Jacob Weinberg was a daring impersonator who fooled people for years, even though it often landed him in prison.

____ ☐ 3. Dressed as a navy officer, Stephen Jacob Weinberg fooled Princess Fatima into paying for his expenses in New York.

____ Score 15 points for a correct *M* answer.
____ Score 5 points for each correct *B* or *N* answer.

____ TOTAL SCORE: Finding the Main Idea

B RECALLING FACTS

How well do you remember the facts in the story you just read? Put an *x* in the box in front of the correct answer to each of the multiple-choice questions below.

1. A shop owner recognized Weinberg as the
   ___ ☐ a. person who set fire to his store.
   ___ ☐ b. thief who stole a camera from him.
   ___ ☐ c. man who pretended to be a lawyer.

2. Posing as Dr. Wyman, Weinberg was sent to
   ___ ☐ a. Peru.
   ___ ☐ b. Serbia.
   ___ ☐ c. Morocco.

3. Princess Fatima of Afghanistan hoped to meet
   ___ ☐ a. the mayor of New York City.
   ___ ☐ b. Stephen Jacob Weinberg.
   ___ ☐ c. President Warren Harding.

4. Erwin News Service hired Weinberg to report on
   ___ ☐ a. World War II.
   ___ ☐ b. the United Nations.
   ___ ☐ c. local news from New York City.

5. The State Department discovered that Weinberg had been offered the job of press officer in Thailand when he
   ___ ☐ a. wrote them a letter.
   ___ ☐ b. applied for a passport.
   ___ ☐ c. announced it on the radio.

Score 5 points for each correct answer.

___ TOTAL SCORE: Recalling Facts

C MAKING INFERENCES

When you use information from the text and your own experience to draw a conclusion that is not directly stated in the text, you are making an *inference*.

Below are five statements that may or may *not* be inferences based on the facts of the story. Write the letter *C* in the box in front of each statement that is a correct inference. Write the letter *F* in front of each faulty inference.

C—Correct Inference   F—Faulty Inference

___ ☐ 1. Many people are willing to believe what a stranger says, even when the stranger is lying.

___ ☐ 2. No matter whom he was pretending to be, Weinberg seemed honest and self-confident.

___ ☐ 3. A real doctor can always recognize another real doctor.

___ ☐ 4. During World War II, men with certain physical disabilities were not required to serve in the army.

___ ☐ 5. Time spent in prison always convinces criminals to change their ways.

Score 5 points for each correct *C* or *F* answer.

___ TOTAL SCORE: Making Inferences

D USING WORDS PRECISELY

Each numbered sentence below contains an underlined word or phrase from the story you have just read. Following the sentence are three definitions. One is a *synonym* for the underlined word, one is an *antonym*, and one has a completely *different* meaning than the underlined word.

For each definition, write the letter that stands for the correct answer in the box.

S—Synonym   A—Antonym   D—Different

1. For a while, he <u>posed as</u> an army officer from Serbia.

____ ☐ a. followed

____ ☐ b. really became

____ ☐ c. pretended to be

2. By 1920 Weinberg was ready for another <u>challenge</u>.

____ ☐ a. easy task

____ ☐ b. crime

____ ☐ c. difficult task

3. He simply <u>approved</u> everything they did.

____ ☐ a. accepted

____ ☐ b. found fault with

____ ☐ c. assigned

4. She finally smartened up when "Wyman" offered to help her sell her <u>priceless</u> forty-two-carat diamond.

____ ☐ a. precious

____ ☐ b. very old

____ ☐ c. worthless

5. "Weyman" had <u>convinced them</u> that he had worked as a spy on their behalf during World War II.

____ ☐ a. caused them to doubt

____ ☐ b. made them believe

____ ☐ c. blamed them

____ Score 3 points for a correct *S* answer.
____ Score 1 point for each correct *A* or *D* answer.

____ TOTAL SCORE: Using Words Precisely

• *Enter the total score for each exercise in the spaces below. Then add the scores together to find your Critical Reading Score. Record your Critical Reading Score on the graph on page 114.*

_____ Finding the Main Idea
_____ Recalling Facts
_____ Making Inferences
_____ Using Words Precisely

_____ CRITICAL READING SCORE: Unit 12

When Andrew Borden and his wife, Abby, were found murdered in their home, suspicion focused on their younger daughter, Lizzie. Although Lizzie and her sister, Emma, both hated their stepmother, only Lizzie was prosecuted for the murders in a celebrated trial.

WAS LIZZIE BORDEN AN AXE MURDERER?

Lizzie Borden took an axe
And gave her mother forty whacks.
When she saw what she had done,
She gave her father forty-one.

This rhyme has been around for more than a hundred years. It describes Lizzie Borden as a cold-blooded killer. But is the rhyme accurate? Did Lizzie butcher her parents one hot August morning in 1892? Or did someone else commit the brutal murders?

The crimes took place in Fall River, Massachusetts. That's where thirty-two-year-old Lizzie Borden lived with her father, stepmother, and older sister, Emma. The morning of August 4, 1892, began quietly enough in the Borden house. Mr. Borden left for work around 9 A.M. Mrs. Borden started to do her housework. The maid, Bridget Sullivan, went outside to wash windows. Emma was away. She was visiting friends in a nearby town. And Lizzie? Well, Lizzie said she spent much of the morning out in the barn. She was getting things ready for a fishing trip she planned to take. The rest of the time, she said, she was in her room, lying down.

Sometime between 9 and 9:30 A.M., Mrs. Borden was making a bed in a second-floor bedroom. Someone crept into the room behind her. Without warning, the killer brought an axe down on Mrs. Borden's head. Nineteen times she was struck with the axe. Blood splattered all over the walls. By the time the killer was finished, Mrs. Borden lay dead. Her body was not found right away, however. When Mr. Borden came home around 10:30 A.M., he had no idea that anything was wrong.

Mr. Borden headed straight for the couch in the sitting room. He had not been feeling well, and the sweltering heat of the morning had drained his energy. He wanted to rest awhile. The maid was also feeling sick that day. A nap sounded like a good idea to her, too. Accordingly, Bridget Sullivan went up to her attic room and quickly fell asleep.

Once again the killer sprang into action. Before Mr. Borden knew what was happening, an axe struck him in the face. The killer delivered ten blows, leaving Mr. Borden—like his wife—dead in the house.

At 11:15 A.M. Lizzie Borden screamed to Bridget Sullivan. "Come down quick! Someone's killed Father!" With those words, Lizzie announced the horrible news. Soon neighbors, police officers, and reporters were swarming around the Borden home. One of the neighbors discovered Mrs. Borden's body in the upstairs bedroom. By evening, Lizzie's sister Emma had heard the news. She hurried home to be with Lizzie.

Meanwhile, questions swirled through the community. Who could have done such terrible deeds? And why? Suspicion centered on Lizzie. Her story didn't make sense. She said she had been out in the barn, but there were no footprints on the dusty barn floor. It looked to police as though no one had set foot in there for days or even weeks. In addition, the maid reported an interesting detail. When Mr. Borden came home that morning, Lizzie had stood at the top of the stairs, laughing in an odd way. And several hours after the murders, Lizzie was seen burning a piece of wood that looked like an axe handle.

Besides, many people whispered, no one else could have done it. The doors to the house were locked, so no intruder could have gotten in. Everyone knew that Lizzie hated her stepmother. And with Mr. and Mrs. Borden both dead, Lizzie and her sister would inherit half a million dollars.

Yet some questions could not be answered. There was blood all over the crime scenes. So how could it be that no blood was found on Lizzie or her clothing? If Lizzie were the killer, where had she hidden the murder weapon? And how could she have stayed so calm during the hour between the two killings?

Some people decided that Lizzie's sister, Emma, was the murderer. She, too, hated her stepmother. In fact, Emma hated Mrs. Borden even more than Lizzie did. Lizzie was just a baby when her real mother died. But Emma was eleven years old. She was old enough to remember her mother—and to hate the woman who tried to replace her. Like Lizzie, Emma knew she would get a lot of money when her parents died. And although Emma had been staying with friends on the day of the murders, she could easily have sneaked back into town. She had

a key to the house. She would have had no trouble unlocking the door.

Other people believed both sisters were innocent. After all, neither one had ever been violent before. They had always been kind and gentle. The Borden house had been broken into a few months earlier. Perhaps the thief had returned, this time with murder in mind. Or what about the enemies Mr. Borden had made in his business dealings? The killer could have been someone seeking revenge. A stranger *could* have slipped into the house while Lizzie was in the barn. During that time, the door was unlocked.

The police were in a difficult spot. The entire nation was watching the events in Fall River. Most police officers believed Lizzie was the killer. But they had no witness, no murder weapon, and no real evidence. It would be hard to make a case. Still, there was tremendous pressure on them to make an arrest. One week after the killings, they did. They arrested Lizzie Borden and charged her with two counts of murder.

The trial took place in June of 1893. It lasted thirteen days. Both sides did their best. But in the end, the jury simply could not believe that

the calm, quiet Lizzie Borden had committed such awful acts. They spent one hour discussing the case. Then they found Lizzie not guilty.

In many ways, though, the jury's verdict did not matter. Lizzie's life was changed forever. Most people believed she was guilty. To this day, Lizzie Borden is not remembered for her love of animals. She is not remembered for the money she gave to the poor. She is remembered only as the woman who gave her mother "forty whacks" and then went on to give her father "forty-one."

If you have been timed while reading this selection, enter your reading time below. Then turn to the Words-per-Minute table on page 112 and look up your reading speed (words per minute). Enter your reading speed on the graph on page 113.

READING TIME: Unit 13	
_____ : _____	
Minutes	*Seconds*

How Well Did You Read?

- *Complete the four exercises that follow. The directions for each exercise will tell you how to mark your answers.*

- *When you have finished all four exercises, use the answer key on page 108 to check your work. For each right answer, put a check mark (✓) on the line beside the box. For each wrong answer, write the correct answer on the line.*

- *Follow the directions after each exercise to find your scores.*

A FINDING THE MAIN IDEA

A good main idea statement answers two questions: it tells *who* or *what* is the subject of the story, and it answers the understood question *does what?* or *is what?* Look at the three statements below. One expresses the main idea of the story you just read. Another statement is *too broad*; it is vague and doesn't tell much about the topic of the story. The third statement is *too narrow*; it tells about only one part of the story.

Match the statements with the three answer choices below by writing the letter of each answer in the box in front of the statement it goes with.

M—Main Idea   B—Too Broad   N—Too Narrow

____ ☐ 1. One of the most famous unsolved mysteries in Massachusetts is the murder of Lizzie Borden's parents in 1892.

____ ☐ 2. To many people, Lizzie Borden seemed guilty of murdering her parents because her story about where she was when the crimes occurred didn't make sense.

____ ☐ 3. Although Lizzie Borden was tried for the 1892 murder of her parents, there was never any solid evidence that she was guilty.

____ Score 15 points for a correct *M* answer.
____ Score 5 points for each correct *B* or *N* answer.

____ TOTAL SCORE: Finding the Main Idea

B RECALLING FACTS

How well do you remember the facts in the story you just read? Put an *x* in the box in front of the correct answer to each of the multiple-choice questions below.

1. The murders at the Borden home occurred
   - ☐ a. on a hot August morning.
   - ☐ b. during a hot August night.
   - ☐ c. shortly after Mr. Borden remarried.

2. The murderer killed Mr. Borden
   - ☐ a. when he discovered Mrs. Borden's body.
   - ☐ b. during an argument.
   - ☐ c. as he slept on the couch.

3. The maid reported that Lizzie had
   - ☐ a. laughed strangely that morning.
   - ☐ b. been out in the barn.
   - ☐ c. lost her keys to the house.

4. People who blamed the Borden sisters for their parents' murders did NOT give this as a reason:
   - ☐ a. a desire to inherit Mr. Borden's wealth.
   - ☐ b. revenge for driving away their boyfriends.
   - ☐ c. hatred for their stepmother.

5. At Lizzie's trial, the verdict was
   - ☐ a. not guilty.
   - ☐ b. not guilty, on grounds of insanity.
   - ☐ c. thrown out because of prejudice on the part of the jury.

Score 5 points for each correct answer.

____ TOTAL SCORE: Recalling Facts

C MAKING INFERENCES

When you use information from the text and your own experience to draw a conclusion that is not directly stated in the text, you are making an *inference*.

Below are five statements that may or may *not* be inferences based on the facts of the story. Write the letter *C* in the box in front of each statement that is a correct inference. Write the letter *F* in front of each faulty inference.

C—Correct Inference   F—Faulty Inference

1. Whoever killed Mr. and Mrs. Borden had to be strong and able to move quietly.

2. For a long time before the murders, there had been great unhappiness in the Borden household.

3. The members of the jury at Lizzie's trial were divided by the evidence and had to discuss several issues in depth before they came to an agreement.

4. An innocent person accused of a famous crime can be confident that once a jury finds him or her not guilty, the public will accept that verdict.

5. The public's desire to learn every detail of a well-known crime is nothing new.

Score 5 points for each correct *C* or *F* answer.

____ TOTAL SCORE: Making Inferences

D USING WORDS PRECISELY

Each numbered sentence below contains an underlined word or phrase from the story you have just read. Following the sentence are three definitions. One is a *synonym* for the underlined word, one is an *antonym*, and one has a completely *different* meaning than the underlined word.

For each definition, write the letter that stands for the correct answer in the box.

S—Synonym   A—Antonym   D—Different

1. It describes Lizzie Borden as a <u>cold-blooded</u> killer.
   ____ ☐ a. habitually late
   ____ ☐ b. extremely tenderhearted and emotional
   ____ ☐ c. without normal human feelings of pity and kindness

2. Or did someone else commit the <u>brutal</u> murders?
   ____ ☐ a. extremely cruel
   ____ ☐ b. local
   ____ ☐ c. kind

3. Meanwhile, questions <u>swirled</u> through the community.
   ____ ☐ a. moved in a straight line
   ____ ☐ b. waited
   ____ ☐ c. whirled

4. <u>Suspicion</u> centered on Lizzie.
   ____ ☐ a. distrust
   ____ ☐ b. faith
   ____ ☐ c. excitement

5. The doors to the house were locked, so no <u>intruder</u> could have gotten in.
   ____ ☐ a. one who belongs
   ____ ☐ b. unwanted outsider
   ____ ☐ c. instructor

____ Score 3 points for a correct *S* answer.
____ Score 1 point for each correct *A* or *D* answer.

____ TOTAL SCORE: Using Words Precisely

• *Enter the total score for each exercise in the spaces below. Then add the scores together to find your Critical Reading Score. Record your Critical Reading Score on the graph on page 114.*

_____	Finding the Main Idea
_____	Recalling Facts
_____	Making Inferences
_____	Using Words Precisely
_____	CRITICAL READING SCORE: Unit 13

Protected by a wall of bulletproof glass, former Nazi Adolf Eichmann listens to testimony of concentration camp survivors during his trial for the murder of six million people.

THE CAPTURE AND TRIAL OF A NAZI WAR CRIMINAL

On the list of the world's worst criminals, Adolf Eichmann has to rank near the top. He was not just an ordinary criminal. He was a *war* criminal. Eichmann sent six million people to their deaths during World War II. Most frightening of all is that in his own warped mind, Eichmann thought he was doing the right thing.

Eichmann's road to evil began in 1932. That was when he joined the Nazi party. The Nazis were led by Adolf Hitler, a vile madman who wanted to take over Europe. Along the way, Hitler hoped to wipe out all the Jews living there. Eichmann worked his way up in Germany's Nazi party. He rose to a position of great power. He became a specialist in what Hitler called the "Jewish problem." In other words, Eichmann was in charge of killing Jews.

Eichmann carried out his hateful work from 1938 to 1945. These were the years just before and during World War II. During this time, Germany controlled most of Europe. So millions of Jews from France to Poland came under Nazi rule. Eichmann began rounding them up and sending them

to their deaths. "When I am finished with my work," he once bragged, "there will be no more Jews in Europe."

Eichmann shipped his victims to concentration camps. There, anyone who was not able to work was immediately killed. The old, the young, and the sick were sent directly to gas chambers. The rest were forced to work like slaves. A sign over the gate of one camp read, Work Brings Freedom. That was a cruel hoax. The Nazis' real goal was to work Jews until they couldn't work anymore. Then those Jews, too, were killed. By 1945 Adolf Eichmann and his henchmen had murdered six million Jews.

Hitler and the Nazis were finally defeated in 1945. As the war ended, Adolf Hitler killed himself. Other Nazi leaders were caught and put on trial for their war crimes. Most were hanged. But a few top Nazi leaders got away. One of them was Eichmann. In a strange twist of fate, Eichmann *was* captured at first. But no one knew who he was. He had disguised himself in a uniform stolen from a dead German soldier. He was put in a

prisoner-of-war camp along with other low-ranking German soldiers. Before anyone figured out his true identity, he escaped.

The police from many countries searched for Eichmann. He was at the top of the Most Wanted War Criminal list. Still, no one could find him. He had vanished. After a few years, most people stopped looking. But Jewish investigators never gave up. From 1945 on, they continued their search. In 1948 Jews created their own nation, called Israel. The Israeli police sent secret agents around the world looking for Eichmann. For many years, they had no luck. Then in 1960 they got a break. Someone looking just like Eichmann was spotted in South America.

Israel sent secret agents to Buenos Aires, the capital of Argentina. They tracked down the man in question. It *was* Eichmann! He was living under the name Ricardo Clement and working in a local auto plant. The agents were eager to grab him. They wanted to take him to Israel to stand trial for his war crimes. But they had to be careful. If Eichmann realized

93

they were on his trail, he might disappear again. Then they would have to start the search all over.

There was one other problem. Israel had no treaty with Argentina about turning over war criminals. So Argentine police could not be counted on to help the Israeli agents. In fact, the police might try to protect Eichmann. The Israelis decided they would have to kidnap Eichmann. Then somehow they would smuggle him out of the country.

On May 11, 1960, the agents set their trap. They followed Eichmann as he left work. As he walked down the street, a car pulled up beside him and suddenly stopped. Four men jumped out. Eichmann saw them and started to scream. But one of the agents clubbed him over the head. The agents tossed the unconscious Eichmann into the backseat of the car, and the car sped away. The agents then sent a secret message back to Israel: "The beast is in chains."

The agents took Eichmann to a hideout a few miles from Buenos Aires. Eichmann thought they were going to murder him on the spot. "Don't kill me!" he begged. "Please don't kill me!" But the agents had no intention of killing Eichmann. Instead, on May 19, they slipped him onto a chartered plane and took off for Israel.

Eichmann's trial began on April 11, 1961. It lasted several months. During the trial, Eichmann was kept in a bulletproof glass cage in the courtroom. The Israelis put him there to keep him alive. They didn't want anyone to shoot him before the trial was over.

Hundreds of witnesses were called. Many were Jews who had survived Eichmann's death camps. Still, Eichmann maintained he was not guilty. He argued that he had not personally killed anyone. He had simply arranged to send Jews to the camps. It was not his fault, he said, that they had been killed there. Besides, he protested, he was simply following orders. Wasn't that what good soldiers were supposed to do?

No one accepted these excuses. The whole world knew what Adolf Eichmann had done. On December 15, 1961, the court announced its verdict. Eichmann, his face pale and twitchy, rose to hear the words of Judge Moshe Landau: "The court finds you guilty."

The court convicted Eichmann of war crimes. It also found him guilty of crimes against humanity and crimes against the Jewish people. The judges rejected Eichmann's claim that he was just following orders. As Judge Landau said, Eichmann was not "a puppet in the hands of others. He was among those who pulled the strings. This block of ice . . . this block of marble . . . closed his ears to the voice of his conscience."

Judge Landau asked Eichmann if he had anything to say. In Eichmann's final statement, he said, "I am not the monster I am made out to be."

The court—and the world—disagreed. Judges sentenced Adolf Eichmann to be hanged. The sentence was carried out on May 31, 1962. The man who had once claimed to be the "World's Number One Jew Killer" had finally been brought to justice.

If you have been timed while reading this selection, enter your reading time below. Then turn to the Words-per-Minute table on page 112 and look up your reading speed (words per minute). Enter your reading speed on the graph on page 113.

READING TIME: Unit 14
_____ : _____
Minutes   *Seconds*

How Well Did You Read?

- *Complete the four exercises that follow. The directions for each exercise will tell you how to mark your answers.*

- *When you have finished all four exercises, use the answer key on page 108 to check your work. For each right answer, put a check mark (✓) on the line beside the box. For each wrong answer, write the correct answer on the line.*

- *Follow the directions after each exercise to find your scores.*

A FINDING THE MAIN IDEA

A good main idea statement answers two questions: it tells *who* or *what* is the subject of the story, and it answers the understood question *does what?* or *is what?* Look at the three statements below. One expresses the main idea of the story you just read. Another statement is *too broad*; it is vague and doesn't tell much about the topic of the story. The third statement is *too narrow*; it tells about only one part of the story.

Match the statements with the three answer choices below by writing the letter of each answer in the box in front of the statement it goes with.

M—Main Idea   B—Too Broad   N—Too Narrow

_____ ☐ 1. The crimes committed during World War II will never be forgotten.

_____ ☐ 2. Adolf Eichmann argued that he had not personally killed any Jews and so he was innocent.

_____ ☐ 3. Nazi war criminal Adolf Eichmann learned that there was no escape from justice.

_____ Score 15 points for a correct *M* answer.
_____ Score 5 points for each correct *B* or *N* answer.

_____ TOTAL SCORE: Finding the Main Idea

B RECALLING FACTS

How well do you remember the facts in the story you just read? Put an *x* in the box in front of the correct answer to each of the multiple-choice questions below.

1. Adolf Eichmann was in charge of
   ____ ☐ a. Germany's labor department.
   ____ ☐ b. protecting Adolf Hitler from attack.
   ____ ☐ c. getting rid of Jews.

2. The war in Europe ended when Hitler and the Nazis were defeated in
   ____ ☐ a. 1945.
   ____ ☐ b. 1948.
   ____ ☐ c. 1960.

3. In 1960, Israeli agents found Eichmann living in
   ____ ☐ a. Germany.
   ____ ☐ b. Argentina.
   ____ ☐ c. Israel.

4. Israeli agents captured Eichmann by
   ____ ☐ a. pulling him into a car as he walked down the street.
   ____ ☐ b. having the police arrest him at work.
   ____ ☐ c. surprising him in his home.

5. Israelis protected Eichmann during his trial by
   ____ ☐ a. giving him a bulletproof vest to wear.
   ____ ☐ b. putting him in a bulletproof glass cage.
   ____ ☐ c. not letting him attend the trial.

Score 5 points for each correct answer.

____ TOTAL SCORE: Recalling Facts

C MAKING INFERENCES

When you use information from the text and your own experience to draw a conclusion that is not directly stated in the text, you are making an *inference*.

Below are five statements that may or may *not* be inferences based on the facts of the story. Write the letter *C* in the box in front of each statement that is a correct inference. Write the letter *F* in front of each faulty inference.

C—Correct Inference   F—Faulty Inference

____ ☐ 1. Even during a war, soldiers must follow basic laws of morality.

____ ☐ 2. In the eyes of the Israeli judges, the most important thing for a soldier to do is follow orders.

____ ☐ 3. Adolf Eichmann probably felt deep sorrow and pity for Jews during the war.

____ ☐ 4. Many former Nazis in hiding became nervous about their own safety after Eichmann was arrested and tried.

____ ☐ 5. By 1961 most Jews had forgiven and forgotten the way the Nazis had treated the Jewish people.

Score 5 points for each correct *C* or *F* answer.

____ TOTAL SCORE: Making Inferences

USING WORDS PRECISELY

Each numbered sentence below contains an underlined word or phrase from the story you have just read. Following the sentence are three definitions. One is a *synonym* for the underlined word, one is an *antonym*, and one has a completely *different* meaning than the underlined word.

For each definition, write the letter that stands for the correct answer in the box.

S—Synonym   A—Antonym   D—Different

1. The Nazis were led by Adolf Hitler, a <u>vile</u> madman.

    ____ ☐ a. evil

    ____ ☐ b. eager

    ____ ☐ c. good

2. Most frightening of all is the fact that in his own <u>warped</u> mind, Eichmann thought he was right.

    ____ ☐ a. intelligent

    ____ ☐ b. healthy

    ____ ☐ c. twisted

3. The old, the young, and the sick were sent <u>directly</u> to gas chambers.

    ____ ☐ a. sadly

    ____ ☐ b. straight

    ____ ☐ c. after a long delay

4. He had <u>disguised himself</u> in a uniform stolen from a dead German soldier.

    ____ ☐ a. showed his true identity

    ____ ☐ b. covered up his identity

    ____ ☐ c. brought glory to himself

5. Besides, he <u>protested</u>, he was simply following orders.

    ____ ☐ a. agreed

    ____ ☐ b. laughed

    ____ ☐ c. objected

____ Score 3 points for a correct *S* answer.

____ Score 1 point for each correct *A* or *D* answer.

____ TOTAL SCORE: Using Words Precisely

• *Enter the total score for each exercise in the spaces below. Then add the scores together to find your Critical Reading Score. Record your Critical Reading Score on the graph on page 114.*

_____	Finding the Main Idea
_____	Recalling Facts
_____	Making Inferences
_____	Using Words Precisely
_____	CRITICAL READING SCORE: Unit 14

After his arrest for leaking U.S. military secrets to a foreign government, Jonathan Jay Pollard shows no discomfort or regret. As fascinated as Pollard was with the notion of spying, he may even have enjoyed the attention of the press and public—that is, until he was sentenced to life imprisonment for his espionage.

A TRAITOR TO HIS COUNTRY

Jonathan Jay Pollard didn't kill anyone. He didn't rob any banks or stop any trains. He didn't kidnap a child or set fire to a building. Still, Pollard was a criminal. Some would say he was the worst kind of criminal—a traitor to his country.

Pollard was an American Jew who was born in Texas and reared in Indiana. But the place he really loved was Israel. Many Jews love Israel—it is, after all, a mainly Jewish nation. But most American Jews give their first loyalty to the United States. Pollard was different. He put Israel first. He was ready to do *anything* for Israel—even if it meant betraying the United States.

Pollard went to college in California. He told classmates he was a spy for Israel. He said he had fought for Israel in its 1973 war against the Arabs. Then the Mossad—Israel's spy agency—had hired him. The Mossad had sent him to France, where he had sold arms to China and South Africa. That was quite a record for a student barely twenty years old! But none of it was true. Pollard made up all those stories to impress his friends.

Pollard finished college in 1976. He tried to get a job as a spy for America's Central Intelligence Agency (CIA). In some ways, he looked good. He was smart and well informed about the world. But when CIA officials checked his background, they found out about his spy fantasies. They also learned that Pollard used drugs and drank heavily. So the agency refused to hire him.

Three years later, Pollard applied for a job with the U.S. Navy. The navy, too, did a standard background check on Pollard. This time his problems were not discovered. The agents who did the check got lazy. They didn't dig deep enough to find out about Pollard's lying and drug use. So he got the job. The navy gave him top-secret clearance. That meant Pollard could get his hands on America's most prized secrets.

At that point, Pollard hadn't done any real spying for anyone. But his fantasy life was still in high gear. Pollard began to brag that he knew a top South African official. He claimed that he had lived in South Africa. He even boasted that his father was the

CIA chief in South Africa.

At first, navy officials believed him. But when they pressed for more details, they discovered Pollard was a liar. The navy took away his top-secret clearance. Navy officials told him that he was sick. They urged him to get some help. Pollard did see a therapist. A year later he got back his clearance.

Pollard behaved himself for the next few years. By 1984, however, he was ready to do some real spying. As he later testified, he was upset with American leaders. He felt they were not giving Israel enough help in fighting its enemies. The United States and Israel were close allies. But even the best of friends don't share all their secrets with each other. The United States kept some information from Israel. Pollard wanted to change that.

He got in touch with some top Israeli agents. He told them he was willing to spy for them. He said he could give them important U.S. papers. It was against Israeli law to spy on the United States, but the agents were eager to learn America's secrets. So they took Pollard's offer. They agreed to pay him $1,500 a month for his work.

For the next eighteen months, Pollard kept his job with the U.S. Navy. Throughout that time, he was secretly working for Israel. He smuggled secret maps, photos, and other papers out of his office and gave them to Israeli agents. They then copied the material and returned it to Pollard. He put it back where it belonged before it was missed.

The Israeli agents were happy with Pollard's work. They raised his salary to $2,500 a month. They even promised him a huge payoff. If Pollard spied for nine years, they said, he could move to Israel. They would give him a new identity—Danny Cohen. And they would have $300,000 waiting for him in a Swiss bank.

Meanwhile, Pollard's American bosses were not so happy. They didn't know about Pollard's work for Israel, of course, but they began to question some of Pollard's actions. One boss, Jerry Agee, began watching Pollard closely. He saw that Pollard had "huge stacks" of top-secret papers on his desk. Many had nothing to do with his job. Then, on October 25, 1985, a fellow worker saw Pollard taking secret papers home. Sensing that something was wrong, the worker told Agee what he had seen.

Agee notified the police. Officers began watching Pollard twenty-four hours a day. They used hidden cameras to film his every move. On November 18, they called him in for questioning. During a break, Pollard phoned his wife, Anne. He slipped the word *cactus* into the conversation. That was a code word to her. It meant he was in trouble. Anne took the hint and hid a suitcase full of secret documents. A suspicious neighbor saw her and called the police.

When police saw the documents, they knew that Pollard had been selling secrets—but to whom? To find out, the police pretended they had no further questions for Pollard. They released him. Then they followed him to see where he would go. On November 21, he and his wife headed for the Israeli embassy. They got through the embassy gate, but no further. The guards turned them away. The Israelis had found out that Pollard was being followed. They wanted nothing more to do with him.

At his trial, Jonathan Jay Pollard pleaded guilty. But he also tried to justify his spying. He said that he had acted out of loyalty to Israel. He did not feel he was betraying the United States. He was just helping an American ally. It was not as though he were sending secrets to an enemy nation, he said. For these reasons, Pollard and his wife hoped for light sentences. They were sorely disappointed. Judge Aubrey Robinson believed that a traitor was a traitor, no matter which foreign country was involved. The judge gave Pollard life in prison, and he gave Anne a five-year sentence.

If you have been timed while reading this selection, enter your reading time below. Then turn to the Words-per-Minute table on page 112 and look up your reading speed (words per minute). Enter your reading speed on the graph on page 113.

READING TIME: Unit 15

_____ : _____
Minutes   *Seconds*

How Well Did You Read?

- *Complete the four exercises that follow. The directions for each exercise will tell you how to mark your answers.*

- *When you have finished all four exercises, use the answer key on page 108 to check your work. For each right answer, put a check mark (✓) on the line beside the box. For each wrong answer, write the correct answer on the line.*

- *Follow the directions after each exercise to find your scores.*

A FINDING THE MAIN IDEA

A good main idea statement answers two questions: it tells *who* or *what* is the subject of the story, and it answers the understood question *does what?* or *is what?* Look at the three statements below. One expresses the main idea of the story you just read. Another statement is *too broad*; it is vague and doesn't tell much about the topic of the story. The third statement is *too narrow*; it tells about only one part of the story.

Match the statements with the three answer choices below by writing the letter of each answer in the box in front of the statement it goes with.

M—Main Idea   B—Too Broad   N—Too Narrow

____ ☐ 1. What Jonathan Pollard did was not a crime against other individuals—it was a crime against his country.

____ ☐ 2. When Jonathan Pollard used his position with the navy to betray U.S. secrets to Israel, he thought he was helping an ally.

____ ☐ 3. Jonathan Jay Pollard arranged to use the code word *cactus* to let his wife know that they were in trouble.

____ Score 15 points for a correct *M* answer.
____ Score 5 points for each correct *B* or *N* answer.

____ TOTAL SCORE: Finding the Main Idea

B | RECALLING FACTS

How well do you remember the facts in the story you just read? Put an *x* in the box in front of the correct answer to each of the multiple-choice questions below.

1. Jonathan Jay Pollard was born in
   ____ □ a. Israel.
   ____ □ b. Texas.
   ____ □ c. Russia.

2. While in college, Pollard told friends he had
   ____ □ a. worked for Israel's spy agency.
   ____ □ b. worked for the U.S. Navy.
   ____ □ c. lived in South Africa as a child.

3. The CIA's reasons for refusing a job to Pollard did NOT include
   ____ □ a. fantasies about being a spy.
   ____ □ b. use of drugs and liquor.
   ____ □ c. a criminal record.

4. After Pollard saw a therapist,
   ____ □ a. the navy restored his top-secret clearance.
   ____ □ b. he was able to forget his fantasies.
   ____ □ c. the navy gave him disability pay.

5. The navy began to suspect Pollard when a boss
   ____ □ a. caught him copying top-secret papers.
   ____ □ b. heard him bragging about his activities.
   ____ □ c. saw him looking at top-secret papers that had nothing to do with his work.

Score 5 points for each correct answer

____ TOTAL SCORE: Recalling Facts

C | MAKING INFERENCES

When you use information from the text and your own experience to draw a conclusion that is not directly stated in the text, you are making an *inference*.

Below are five statements that may or may *not* be inferences based on the facts of the story. Write the letter *C* in the box in front of each statement that is a correct inference. Write the letter *F* in front of each faulty inference.

C—Correct Inference   F—Faulty Inference

____ □ 1. Judge Aubrey Robinson believed that when the U.S. government did not do what each citizen wanted done, the citizens were right to take matters into their own hands.

____ □ 2. On their own, Pollard's neighbors had begun to notice that the Pollards were behaving oddly and deserved to be watched.

____ □ 3. Although Pollard insisted he was doing a good thing for an ally, he and his wife knew all along that they were breaking laws.

____ □ 4. For both Pollard and his wife, the money that they received for their spying had absolutely no influence on their decision to spy.

____ □ 5. If Pollard is ever released from prison, Israel's spy agency will be happy to hire him again.

Score 5 points for each correct *C* or *F* answer.

____ TOTAL SCORE: Making Inferences

D USING WORDS PRECISELY

Each numbered sentence below contains an underlined word or phrase from the story you have just read. Following the sentence are three definitions. One is a *synonym* for the underlined word, one is an *antonym*, and one has a completely *different* meaning than the underlined word.

For each definition, write the letter that stands for the correct answer in the box.

S—Synonym   A—Antonym   D—Different

1. But when CIA officials checked his background, they found out about his spy <u>fantasies</u>.

____ ☐ a. tales from one's imagination

____ ☐ b. truths

____ ☐ c. talents

2. The United States and Israel were close <u>allies</u>.

____ ☐ a. friends

____ ☐ b. neighbors

____ ☐ c. enemies

3. He <u>smuggled</u> secret maps, photos, and other papers out of his office and gave them to Israeli agents.

____ ☐ a. paraded

____ ☐ b. recognized

____ ☐ c. carried out in secret

4. At his trial, Jonathan Jay Pollard pleaded guilty. But he also tried to <u>justify</u> his spying.

____ ☐ a. act out

____ ☐ b. prove to be right

____ ☐ c. judge as wrong

5. He did not feel he was <u>betraying</u> the United States.

____ ☐ a. fighting for, defending

____ ☐ b. being false or disloyal to

____ ☐ c. visiting

____ Score 3 points for a correct *S* answer.
____ Score 1 point for each correct *A* or *D* answer.

____ TOTAL SCORE: Using Words Precisely

• *Enter the total score for each exercise in the spaces below. Then add the scores together to find your Critical Reading Score. Record your Critical Reading Score on the graph on page 114.*

_____ Finding the Main Idea
_____ Recalling Facts
_____ Making Inferences
_____ Using Words Precisely

_____ CRITICAL READING SCORE: Unit 15

Answer Key

1 Bonnie and Clyde
Pages 10–15

A. Finding the Main Idea
1. B   2. N   3. M

B. Recalling Facts
1. b   2. a   3. c   4. b   5. c

C. Making Inferences
1. F   2. F   3. F   4. C   5. F

D. Using Words Precisely
1. a. S   b. D   c. A
2. a. A   b. S   c. D
3. a. A   b. D   c. S
4. a. A   b. S   c. D
5. a. A   b. D   c. S

2 Izzy and Moe: Two Honest Men
Pages 16–21

A. Finding the Main Idea
1. N   2. B   3. M

B. Recalling Facts
1. c   2. a   3. c   4. b   5. b

C. Making Inferences
1. C   2. F   3. F   4. C   5. C

D. Using Words Precisely
1. a. A   b. S   c. D
2. a. S   b. A   c. D
3. a. D   b. S   c. A
4. a. A   b. D   c. S
5. a. S   b. D   c. A

3 The Kidnapping of John Paul Getty III
Pages 22–27

A. Finding the Main Idea
1. M   2. N   3. B

B. Recalling Facts
1. a   2. c   3. c   4. a   5. b

C. Making Inferences
1. C   2. F   3. C   4. F   5. F

D. Using Words Precisely
1. a. S   b. D   c. A
2. a. A   b. D   c. S
3. a. S   b. A   c. D
4. a. A   b. S   c. D
5. a. D   b. A   c. S

4 The Brink's Robbery: The "Perfect" Crime
Pages 28–33

A. Finding the Main Idea
1. B   2. M   3. N

B. Recalling Facts
1. c   2. b   3. a   4. c   5. a

C. Making Inferences
1. C   2. C   3. F   4. F   5. F

D. Using Words Precisely
1. a. A   b. D   c. S
2. a. S   b. A   c. D
3. a. D   b. S   c. A
4. a. A   b. S   c. D
5. a. S   b. D   c. A

5 Punishment, Singapore Style
Pages 34–39

A. Finding the Main Idea
1. B   2. N   3. M

B. Recalling Facts
1. c   2. a   3. b   4. c   5. b

C. Making Inferences
1. F   2. C   3. F   4. F   5. C

D. Using Words Precisely
1. a. D   b. S   c. A
2. a. A   b. D   c. S
3. a. A   b. S   c. D
4. a. D   b. A   c. S
5. a. S   b. D   c. A

6 The Real Jesse James
Pages 42-47

A. Finding the Main Idea
   1. M   2. B   3. N

B. Recalling Facts
   1. c   2. c   3. a   4. a   5. b

C. Making Inferences
   1. C   2. F   3. C   4. F   5. C

D. Using Words Precisely
   1. a. S   b. A   c. D
   2. a. A   b. D   c. S
   3. a. D   b. S   c. A
   4. a. A   b. S   c. D
   5. a. D   b. A   c. S

7 Typhoid Mary
Pages 48-53

A. Finding the Main Idea
   1. N   2. B   3. M

B. Recalling Facts
   1. a   2. b   3. c   4. b   5. a

C. Making Inferences
   1. F   2. C   3. C   4. F   5. C

D. Using Words Precisely
   1. a. S   b. A   c. D
   2. a. D   b. S   c. A
   3. a. A   b. D   c. S
   4. a. D   b. S   c. A
   5. a. A   b. S   c. D

8 The Great Train Robbery
Pages 54-59

A. Finding the Main Idea
   1. N   2. M   3. B

B. Recalling Facts
   1. a   2. c   3. c   4. b   5. a

C. Making Inferences
   1. C   2. F   3. F   4. C   5. F

D. Using Words Precisely
   1. a. D   b. A   c. S
   2. a. S   b. D   c. A
   3. a. A   b. D   c. S
   4. a. D   b. S   c. A
   5. a. A   b. S   c. D

9 John Dillinger: A Crook with Style
Pages 60-65

A. Finding the Main Idea
   1. B   2. M   3. N

B. Recalling Facts
   1. c   2. b   3. b   4. c   5. a

C. Making Inferences
   1. C   2. F   3. C   4. F   5. C

D. Using Words Precisely
   1. a. A   b. S   c. D
   2. a. S   b. D   c. A
   3. a. S   b. A   c. D
   4. a. A   b. D   c. S
   5. a. D   b. A   c. S

10 Assassin!
Pages 66-71

A. Finding the Main Idea
   1. M   2. B   3. N

B. Recalling Facts
   1. a   2. c   3. b   4. a   5. c

C. Making Inferences
   1. F   2. F   3. C   4. F   5. C

D. Using Words Precisely
   1. a. A   b. S   c. D
   2. a. S   b. D   c. A
   3. a. D   b. A   c. S
   4. a. S   b. A   c. D
   5. a. D   b. S   c. A

11 Machine Gun Kelly: Public Enemy Number One
Pages 74–79
A. Finding the Main Idea
  1. B 2. N 3. M
B. Recalling Facts
  1. c 2. b 3. c 4. a 5. a
C. Making Inferences
  1. F 2. C 3. F 4. F 5. C
D. Using Words Precisely
  1. a. D b. S c. A
  2. a. S b. A c. D
  3. a. A b. D c. S
  4. a. S b. A c. D
  5. a. A b. D c. S

12 Stephen Jacob Weinberg: The Man with Many Faces
Pages 80–85
A. Finding the Main Idea
  1. B 2. M 3. N
B. Recalling Facts
  1. b 2. a 3. c 4. b 5. a
C. Making Inferences
  1. C 2. C 3. F 4. C 5. F
D. Using Words Precisely
  1. a. D b. A c. S
  2. a. A b. D c. S
  3. a. S b. A c. D
  4. a. S b. D c. A
  5. a. A b. S c. D

13 Was Lizzie Borden an Axe Murderer?
Pages 86–91
A. Finding the Main Idea
  1. B 2. N 3. M
B. Recalling Facts
  1. a 2. c 3. a 4. b 5. a
C. Making Inferences
  1. C 2. C 3. F 4. F 5. C
D. Using Words Precisely
  1. a. D b. A c. S
  2. a. S b. D c. A
  3. a. A b. D c. S
  4. a. S b. A c. D
  5. a. A b. S c. D

14 The Capture and Trial of a Nazi War Criminal
Pages 92–97
A. Finding the Main Idea
  1. B 2. N 3. M
B. Recalling Facts
  1. c 2. a 3. b 4. a 5. b
C. Making Inferences
  1. C 2. F 3. F 4. C 5. F
D. Using Words Precisely
  1. a. S b. D c. A
  2. a. D b. A c. S
  3. a. D b. S c. A
  4. a. A b. S c. D
  5. a. A b. D c. S

15 A Traitor to His Country
Pages 98–103
A. Finding the Main Idea
  1. B 2. M 3. N
B. Recalling Facts
  1. b 2. a 3. c 4. a 5. c
C. Making Inferences
  1. F 2. C 3. C 4. F 5. F
D. Using Words Precisely
  1. a. S b. A c. D
  2. a. S b. D c. A
  3. a. A b. D c. S
  4. a. D b. S c. A
  5. a. A b. S c. D

Words-per-Minute Tables
and Progress Graphs

WORDS PER MINUTE

Unit ▶	Sample	1	2	3	4	5	
No. of Words ▶	632	1120	838	884	1069	982	
1:30	421	747	559	589	713	655	**90**
1:40	379	672	503	530	641	589	**100**
1:50	345	611	457	482	583	536	**110**
2:00	316	560	419	442	535	491	**120**
2:10	292	517	387	408	493	453	**130**
2:20	271	480	359	379	458	421	**140**
2:30	253	448	335	354	428	393	**150**
2:40	237	420	314	332	401	368	**160**
2:50	223	395	296	312	377	347	**170**
3:00	211	373	279	295	356	327	**180**
3:10	200	354	265	279	338	310	**190**
3:20	190	336	251	265	321	295	**200**
3:30	181	320	239	253	305	281	**210**
3:40	172	305	229	241	292	268	**220**
3:50	165	292	219	231	279	256	**230**
4:00	158	280	210	221	267	246	**240**
4:10	152	269	201	212	257	236	**250**
4:20	146	258	193	204	247	227	**260**
4:30	140	249	186	196	238	218	**270**
4:40	135	240	180	189	229	210	**280**
4:50	131	232	173	183	221	203	**290**
5:00	126	224	168	177	214	196	**300**
5:10	122	217	162	171	207	190	**310**
5:20	119	210	157	166	200	184	**320**
5:30	115	204	152	161	194	179	**330**
5:40	112	198	148	156	189	173	**340**
5:50	108	192	144	152	183	168	**350**
6:00	105	187	140	147	178	164	**360**
6:10	102	182	136	143	173	159	**370**
6:20	100	177	132	140	169	155	**380**
6:30	97	172	129	136	164	151	**390**
6:40	95	168	126	133	160	147	**400**
6:50	92	164	123	129	156	144	**410**
7:00	90	160	120	126	153	140	**420**
7:10	88	156	117	123	149	137	**430**
7:20	86	153	114	121	146	134	**440**
7:30	84	149	112	118	143	131	**450**
7:40	82	146	109	115	139	128	**460**
7:50	81	143	107	113	136	125	**470**
8:00	79	140	105	111	134	123	**480**

GROUP ONE

Minutes and Seconds ▶   ◀ *Seconds*

Unit ➤	6	7	8	9	10	
No. of Words ➤	1053	916	854	1045	1008	
1:30	702	611	569	697	672	**90**
1:40	632	550	512	627	605	**100**
1:50	574	500	466	570	550	**110**
2:00	527	458	427	523	504	**120**
2:10	486	423	394	482	465	**130**
2:20	451	393	366	448	432	**140**
2:30	421	366	342	418	403	**150**
2:40	395	344	320	392	378	**160**
2:50	372	323	301	369	356	**170**
3:00	351	305	285	348	336	**180**
3:10	333	289	270	330	318	**190**
3:20	316	275	256	314	302	**200**
3:30	301	262	244	299	288	**210**
3:40	287	250	233	285	275	**220**
3:50	275	239	223	273	263	**230**
4:00	263	229	214	261	252	**240**
4:10	253	220	205	251	242	**250**
4:20	243	211	197	241	233	**260**
4:30	234	204	190	232	224	**270**
4:40	226	196	183	224	216	**280**
4:50	218	190	177	216	209	**290**
5:00	211	183	171	209	202	**300**
5:10	204	177	165	202	195	**310**
5:20	197	172	160	196	189	**320**
5:30	191	167	155	190	183	**330**
5:40	186	162	151	184	178	**340**
5:50	181	157	146	179	173	**350**
6:00	176	153	142	174	168	**360**
6:10	171	149	138	169	163	**370**
6:20	166	145	135	165	159	**380**
6:30	162	141	131	161	155	**390**
6:40	158	137	128	157	151	**400**
6:50	154	134	125	153	148	**410**
7:00	150	131	122	149	144	**420**
7:10	147	128	119	146	141	**430**
7:20	144	125	116	143	137	**440**
7:30	140	122	114	139	134	**450**
7:40	137	119	111	136	131	**460**
7:50	134	117	109	133	129	**470**
8:00	132	115	107	131	126	**480**

Minutes and Seconds ➤

◄ *Seconds*

GROUP THREE

Minutes and Seconds	11	12	13	14	15	Seconds
No. of Words ➤	846	811	928	871	1094	
1:30	564	541	619	581	729	90
1:40	508	487	557	523	656	100
1:50	461	442	506	475	597	110
2:00	423	406	464	436	547	120
2:10	390	374	428	402	505	130
2:20	363	348	398	373	469	140
2:30	338	324	371	348	438	150
2:40	317	304	348	327	410	160
2:50	299	286	328	307	386	170
3:00	282	270	309	290	365	180
3:10	267	256	293	275	345	190
3:20	254	243	278	261	328	200
3:30	242	232	265	249	313	210
3:40	231	221	253	238	298	220
3:50	221	212	242	227	285	230
4:00	212	203	232	218	274	240
4:10	203	195	223	209	263	250
4:20	195	187	214	201	252	260
4:30	188	180	206	194	243	270
4:40	181	174	199	187	234	280
4:50	175	168	192	180	226	290
5:00	169	162	186	174	219	300
5:10	164	157	180	169	212	310
5:20	159	152	174	163	205	320
5:30	154	147	169	158	199	330
5:40	149	143	164	154	193	340
5:50	145	139	159	149	188	350
6:00	141	135	155	145	182	360
6:10	137	132	150	141	177	370
6:20	134	128	147	138	173	380
6:30	130	125	143	134	168	390
6:40	127	122	139	131	164	400
6:50	124	119	136	127	160	410
7:00	121	116	133	124	156	420
7:10	118	113	129	122	153	430
7:20	115	111	127	119	149	440
7:30	113	108	124	116	146	450
7:40	110	106	121	114	143	460
7:50	108	104	118	111	140	470
8:00	106	101	116	109	137	480

READING SPEED

Directions: *Write your Words-per-Minute score for each unit in the box under the number of the unit. Then plot your reading speed on the graph by putting a small* **x** *on the line directly above the number of the unit, across from the number of words per minute you read. As you mark your speed for each unit, graph your progress by drawing a line to connect the* **x***'s.*

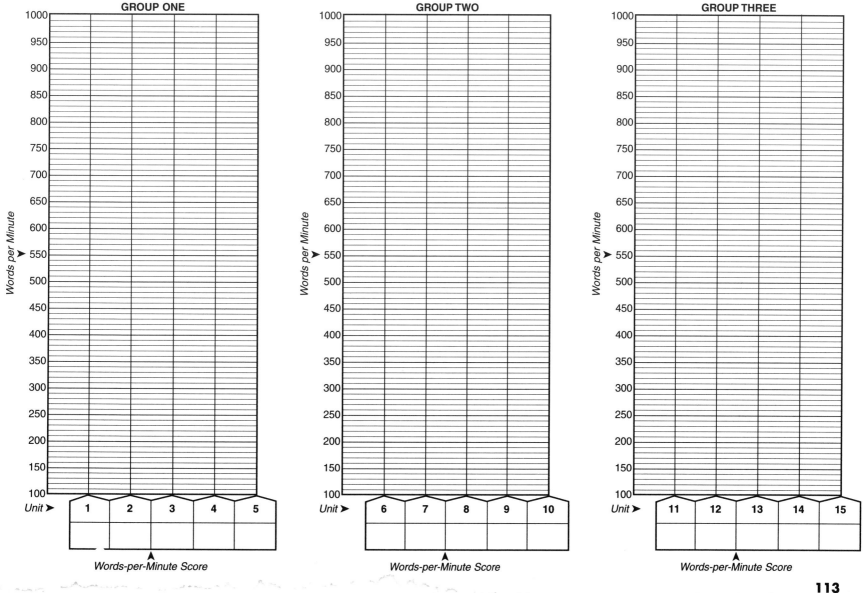

GROUP ONE

GROUP TWO

GROUP THREE

Words per Minute

Unit ➤ | 1 | 2 | 3 | 4 | 5

Words-per-Minute Score

Unit ➤ | 6 | 7 | 8 | 9 | 10

Words-per-Minute Score

Unit ➤ | 11 | 12 | 13 | 14 | 15

Words-per-Minute Score

113

CRITICAL READING SCORES

Directions: *Write your Critical Reading Score for each unit in the box under the number of the unit. Then plot your score on the graph by putting a small x on the line directly above the number of the unit, across from the score you earned. As you mark your score for each unit, graph your progress by drawing a line to connect the x's.*

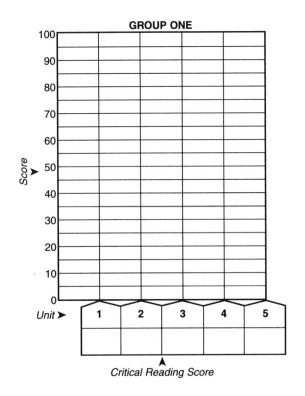

GROUP ONE

Score ➤

Unit ➤ | 1 | 2 | 3 | 4 | 5

Critical Reading Score

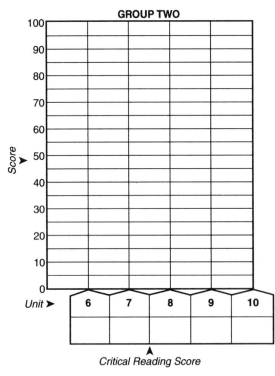

GROUP TWO

Score ➤

Unit ➤ | 6 | 7 | 8 | 9 | 10

Critical Reading Score

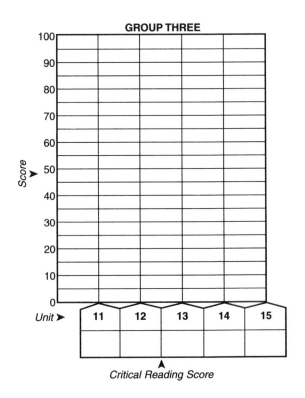

GROUP THREE

Score ➤

Unit ➤ | 11 | 12 | 13 | 14 | 15

Critical Reading Score